Wealth Of Nations

Monthly Success Planner

~ᏕᏗᏲᎡ ᏝᏁᏔᏗ

BUDGET *at a* GLANCE

INCOME SOURCE	AMOUNT	PAYMENT DATE	COMMENTS
INCOME TOTALS			

EXPENSES	AMOUNT	DUE DATE	COMMENTS
Housing			
mortgage/rent			
second mortgage			
property taxes			
home insurance			
maintenance/repairs			
alarm system			
Utilities			
electricity			
heat			
water/sewer			
garbage pick-up			
home phone			
internet			
cable/satellite			
cell phones			
Food			
groceries			
meals out			

Monthly Financial Goals

What improvements can be made from last month? ______________________________

Goals For This Month:

1. ______________________________
2. ______________________________
3. ______________________________

To reach these goals I need to:

- [ ] ______________________________
- [ ] ______________________________
- [ ] ______________________________
- [ ] ______________________________
- [ ] ______________________________
- [ ] ______________________________
- [ ] ______________________________
- [ ] ______________________________

Notes:

BUDGET at a GLANCE

INCOME SOURCE	AMOUNT	PAYMENT DATE	COMMENTS
INCOME TOTALS			

EXPENSES	AMOUNT	DUE DATE	COMMENTS
Housing			
mortgage/rent			
second mortgage			
property taxes			
home insurance			
maintenance/repairs			
alarm system			
Utilities			
electricity			
heat			
water/sewer			
garbage pick-up			
home phone			
internet			
cable/satellite			
cell phones			
Food			
groceries			
meals out			

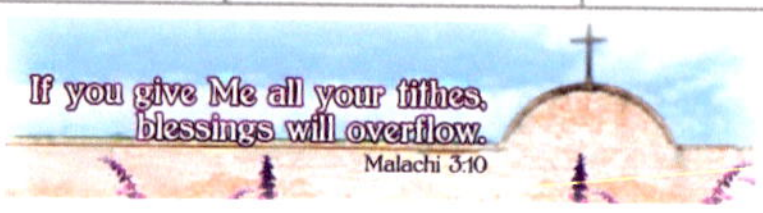

Monthly Financial Goals

What improvements can be made from last month? ______________________

Goals For This Month:

1. ______________________
2. ______________________
3. ______________________

To reach these goals I need to:

- [ ] ______________________
- [ ] ______________________
- [ ] ______________________
- [ ] ______________________
- [ ] ______________________
- [ ] ______________________
- [ ] ______________________
- [ ] ______________________

Notes:

BUDGET at a GLANCE

INCOME SOURCE	AMOUNT	PAYMENT DATE	COMMENTS
INCOME TOTALS			

EXPENSES	AMOUNT	DUE DATE	COMMENTS
Housing			
mortgage/rent			
second mortgage			
property taxes			
home insurance			
maintenance/repairs			
alarm system			
Utilities			
electricity			
heat			
water/sewer			
garbage pick-up			
home phone			
internet			
cable/satellite			
cell phones			
Food			
groceries			
meals out			

Monthly Financial Goals

What improvements can be made from last month? ____________________

Goals For This Month:

1. ____________________
2. ____________________
3. ____________________

To reach these goals I need to:

- [ ] ____________________
- [ ] ____________________
- [ ] ____________________
- [ ] ____________________
- [ ] ____________________
- [ ] ____________________
- [ ] ____________________
- [ ] ____________________

Notes:

BUDGET at a GLANCE

INCOME SOURCE	AMOUNT	PAYMENT DATE	COMMENTS
INCOME TOTALS			

EXPENSES	AMOUNT	DUE DATE	COMMENTS
Housing			
mortgage/rent			
second mortgage			
property taxes			
home insurance			
maintenance/repairs			
alarm system			
Utilities			
electricity			
heat			
water/sewer			
garbage pick-up			
home phone			
internet			
cable/satellite			
cell phones			
Food			
groceries			
meals out			

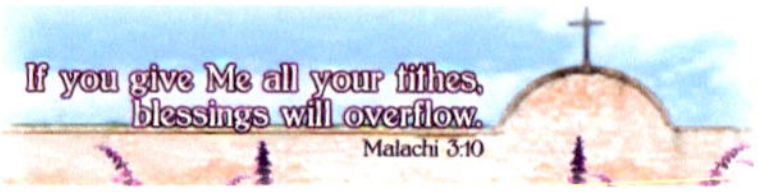

Monthly Financial Goals

What improvements can be made from last month? ____________________

Goals For This Month:

1. ____________________
2. ____________________
3. ____________________

To reach these goals I need to:

- [ ] ____________________
- [ ] ____________________
- [ ] ____________________
- [ ] ____________________
- [ ] ____________________
- [ ] ____________________
- [ ] ____________________
- [ ] ____________________

Notes:

BUDGET at a GLANCE

INCOME SOURCE	AMOUNT	PAYMENT DATE	COMMENTS
INCOME TOTALS			

EXPENSES	AMOUNT	DUE DATE	COMMENTS
Housing			
mortgage/rent			
second mortgage			
property taxes			
home insurance			
maintenance/repairs			
alarm system			
Utilities			
electricity			
heat			
water/sewer			
garbage pick-up			
home phone			
internet			
cable/satellite			
cell phones			
Food			
groceries			
meals out			

Monthly Financial Goals

What improvements can be made from last month? ____________________

Goals For This Month:

1. ____________________
2. ____________________
3. ____________________

To reach these goals I need to:

- [ ] ____________________
- [ ] ____________________
- [ ] ____________________
- [ ] ____________________
- [ ] ____________________
- [ ] ____________________
- [ ] ____________________
- [ ] ____________________

Notes:

BUDGET *at a* GLANCE

INCOME SOURCE	AMOUNT	PAYMENT DATE	COMMENTS
INCOME TOTALS			

EXPENSES	AMOUNT	DUE DATE	COMMENTS
Housing			
mortgage/rent			
second mortgage			
property taxes			
home insurance			
maintenance/repairs			
alarm system			
Utilities			
electricity			
heat			
water/sewer			
garbage pick-up			
home phone			
internet			
cable/satellite			
cell phones			
Food			
groceries			
meals out			

Monthly Financial Goals

What improvements can be made from last month? ____________________

Goals For This Month:

1. ____________________
2. ____________________
3. ____________________

To reach these goals I need to:

- [ ] ____________________
- [ ] ____________________
- [ ] ____________________
- [ ] ____________________
- [ ] ____________________
- [ ] ____________________
- [ ] ____________________
- [ ] ____________________

Notes:

BUDGET at a GLANCE

INCOME SOURCE	AMOUNT	PAYMENT DATE	COMMENTS
INCOME TOTALS			

EXPENSES	AMOUNT	DUE DATE	COMMENTS
Housing			
mortgage/rent			
second mortgage			
property taxes			
home insurance			
maintenance/repairs			
alarm system			
Utilities			
electricity			
heat			
water/sewer			
garbage pick-up			
home phone			
internet			
cable/satellite			
cell phones			
Food			
groceries			
meals out			

Monthly Financial Goals

What improvements can be made from last month? ______________________________

Goals For This Month:

1. ______________________________

2. ______________________________

3. ______________________________

To reach these goals I need to:

- [ ] ______________________________
- [ ] ______________________________
- [ ] ______________________________
- [ ] ______________________________
- [ ] ______________________________
- [ ] ______________________________
- [ ] ______________________________
- [ ] ______________________________

Notes:

BUDGET *at a* GLANCE

INCOME SOURCE	AMOUNT	PAYMENT DATE	COMMENTS
INCOME TOTALS			

EXPENSES	AMOUNT	DUE DATE	COMMENTS
Housing			
mortgage/rent			
second mortgage			
property taxes			
home insurance			
maintenance/repairs			
alarm system			
Utilities			
electricity			
heat			
water/sewer			
garbage pick-up			
home phone			
internet			
cable/satellite			
cell phones			
Food			
groceries			
meals out			

Monthly Financial Goals

What improvements can be made from last month? ____________________

Goals For This Month:

1. ____________________
2. ____________________
3. ____________________

To reach these goals I need to:

- [ ] ____________________
- [ ] ____________________
- [ ] ____________________
- [ ] ____________________
- [ ] ____________________
- [ ] ____________________
- [ ] ____________________
- [ ] ____________________

Notes:

BUDGET at a GLANCE

INCOME SOURCE	AMOUNT	PAYMENT DATE	COMMENTS
INCOME TOTALS			

EXPENSES	AMOUNT	DUE DATE	COMMENTS
Housing			
mortgage/rent			
second mortgage			
property taxes			
home insurance			
maintenance/repairs			
alarm system			
Utilities			
electricity			
heat			
water/sewer			
garbage pick-up			
home phone			
internet			
cable/satellite			
cell phones			
Food			
groceries			
meals out			

Monthly Financial Goals

What improvements can be made from last month? ____________________

Goals For This Month:

1. ____________________
2. ____________________
3. ____________________

To reach these goals I need to:

- [ ] ____________________
- [ ] ____________________
- [ ] ____________________
- [ ] ____________________
- [ ] ____________________
- [ ] ____________________
- [ ] ____________________
- [ ] ____________________

Notes:

BUDGET *at a* GLANCE

INCOME SOURCE	AMOUNT	PAYMENT DATE	COMMENTS
INCOME TOTALS			

EXPENSES	AMOUNT	DUE DATE	COMMENTS
Housing			
mortgage/rent			
second mortgage			
property taxes			
home insurance			
maintenance/repairs			
alarm system			
Utilities			
electricity			
heat			
water/sewer			
garbage pick-up			
home phone			
internet			
cable/satellite			
cell phones			
Food			
groceries			
meals out			

Monthly Financial Goals

What improvements can be made from last month? ____________________

Goals For This Month:

1. ____________________
2. ____________________
3. ____________________

To reach these goals I need to:

- [ ] ____________________
- [ ] ____________________
- [ ] ____________________
- [ ] ____________________
- [ ] ____________________
- [ ] ____________________
- [ ] ____________________
- [ ] ____________________

Notes:

BUDGET at a GLANCE

INCOME SOURCE	AMOUNT	PAYMENT DATE	COMMENTS
INCOME TOTALS			

EXPENSES	AMOUNT	DUE DATE	COMMENTS
Housing			
mortgage/rent			
second mortgage			
property taxes			
home insurance			
maintenance/repairs			
alarm system			
Utilities			
electricity			
heat			
water/sewer			
garbage pick-up			
home phone			
internet			
cable/satellite			
cell phones			
Food			
groceries			
meals out			

Monthly Financial Goals

What improvements can be made from last month? ______________________________

Goals For This Month:

1. ______________________________
2. ______________________________
3. ______________________________

To reach these goals I need to:

- [ ] ______________________________
- [ ] ______________________________
- [ ] ______________________________
- [ ] ______________________________
- [ ] ______________________________
- [ ] ______________________________
- [ ] ______________________________
- [ ] ______________________________

Notes:

BUDGET at a GLANCE

INCOME SOURCE	AMOUNT	PAYMENT DATE	COMMENTS
INCOME TOTALS			

EXPENSES	AMOUNT	DUE DATE	COMMENTS
Housing			
mortgage/rent			
second mortgage			
property taxes			
home insurance			
maintenance/repairs			
alarm system			
Utilities			
electricity			
heat			
water/sewer			
garbage pick-up			
home phone			
internet			
cable/satellite			
cell phones			
Food			
groceries			
meals out			

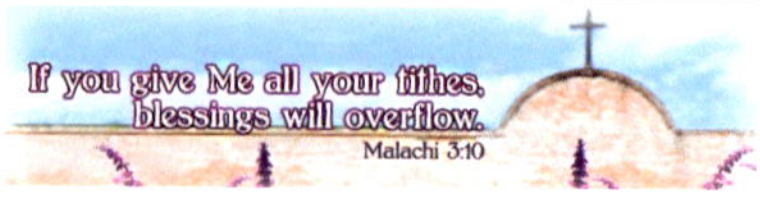

Monthly Financial Goals

What improvements can be made from last month? ______________________________

Goals For This Month:

1. ______________________________
2. ______________________________
3. ______________________________

To reach these goals I need to:

- [ ] ______________________________
- [ ] ______________________________
- [ ] ______________________________
- [ ] ______________________________
- [ ] ______________________________
- [ ] ______________________________
- [ ] ______________________________
- [ ] ______________________________

Notes:

BUDGET at a GLANCE

INCOME SOURCE	AMOUNT	PAYMENT DATE	COMMENTS
INCOME TOTALS			

EXPENSES	AMOUNT	DUE DATE	COMMENTS
Housing			
mortgage/rent			
second mortgage			
property taxes			
home insurance			
maintenance/repairs			
alarm system			
Utilities			
electricity			
heat			
water/sewer			
garbage pick-up			
home phone			
internet			
cable/satellite			
cell phones			
Food			
groceries			
meals out			

Monthly Financial Goals

What improvements can be made from last month? ____________________

Goals For This Month:

1. ____________________
2. ____________________
3. ____________________

To reach these goals I need to:

- [ ] ____________________
- [ ] ____________________
- [ ] ____________________
- [ ] ____________________
- [ ] ____________________
- [ ] ____________________
- [ ] ____________________
- [ ] ____________________

Notes:

BUDGET at a GLANCE

INCOME SOURCE	AMOUNT	PAYMENT DATE	COMMENTS
INCOME TOTALS			

EXPENSES	AMOUNT	DUE DATE	COMMENTS
Housing			
mortgage/rent			
second mortgage			
property taxes			
home insurance			
maintenance/repairs			
alarm system			
Utilities			
electricity			
heat			
water/sewer			
garbage pick-up			
home phone			
internet			
cable/satellite			
cell phones			
Food			
groceries			
meals out			

Monthly Financial Goals

What improvements can be made from last month? ______________________

Goals For This Month:

1. ______________________
2. ______________________
3. ______________________

To reach these goals I need to:

- [ ] ______________________
- [ ] ______________________
- [ ] ______________________
- [ ] ______________________
- [ ] ______________________
- [ ] ______________________
- [ ] ______________________
- [ ] ______________________

Notes:

BUDGET at a GLANCE

INCOME SOURCE	AMOUNT	PAYMENT DATE	COMMENTS
INCOME TOTALS			

EXPENSES	AMOUNT	DUE DATE	COMMENTS
Housing			
mortgage/rent			
second mortgage			
property taxes			
home insurance			
maintenance/repairs			
alarm system			
Utilities			
electricity			
heat			
water/sewer			
garbage pick-up			
home phone			
internet			
cable/satellite			
cell phones			
Food			
groceries			
meals out			

Monthly Financial Goals

What improvements can be made from last month? ______________________________

Goals For This Month:

1. ______________________________

2. ______________________________

3. ______________________________

To reach these goals I need to:

- [ ] ______________________________
- [ ] ______________________________
- [ ] ______________________________
- [ ] ______________________________
- [ ] ______________________________
- [ ] ______________________________
- [ ] ______________________________
- [ ] ______________________________

Notes:

BUDGET *at a* GLANCE

INCOME SOURCE	AMOUNT	PAYMENT DATE	COMMENTS
INCOME TOTALS			

EXPENSES	AMOUNT	DUE DATE	COMMENTS
Housing			
mortgage/rent			
second mortgage			
property taxes			
home insurance			
maintenance/repairs			
alarm system			
Utilities			
electricity			
heat			
water/sewer			
garbage pick-up			
home phone			
internet			
cable/satellite			
cell phones			
Food			
groceries			
meals out			

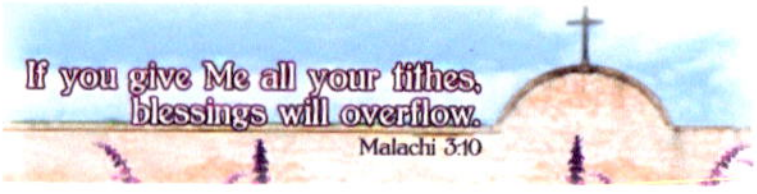

Monthly Financial Goals

What improvements can be made from last month? ______________________

Goals For This Month:

1. ______________________
2. ______________________
3. ______________________

To reach these goals I need to:

- [ ] ______________________
- [ ] ______________________
- [ ] ______________________
- [ ] ______________________
- [ ] ______________________
- [ ] ______________________
- [ ] ______________________
- [ ] ______________________

Notes:

BUDGET at a GLANCE

INCOME SOURCE	AMOUNT	PAYMENT DATE	COMMENTS
INCOME TOTALS			

EXPENSES	AMOUNT	DUE DATE	COMMENTS
Housing			
mortgage/rent			
second mortgage			
property taxes			
home insurance			
maintenance/repairs			
alarm system			
Utilities			
electricity			
heat			
water/sewer			
garbage pick-up			
home phone			
internet			
cable/satellite			
cell phones			
Food			
groceries			
meals out			

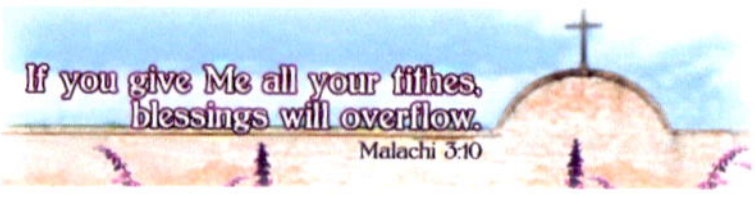

Monthly Financial Goals

What improvements can be made from last month? ______________________

Goals For This Month:

1. ______________________
2. ______________________
3. ______________________

To reach these goals I need to:

- [ ] ______________________
- [ ] ______________________
- [ ] ______________________
- [ ] ______________________
- [ ] ______________________
- [ ] ______________________
- [ ] ______________________
- [ ] ______________________

Notes:

BUDGET at a GLANCE

INCOME SOURCE	AMOUNT	PAYMENT DATE	COMMENTS
INCOME TOTALS			

EXPENSES	AMOUNT	DUE DATE	COMMENTS
Housing			
mortgage/rent			
second mortgage			
property taxes			
home insurance			
maintenance/repairs			
alarm system			
Utilities			
electricity			
heat			
water/sewer			
garbage pick-up			
home phone			
internet			
cable/satellite			
cell phones			
Food			
groceries			
meals out			

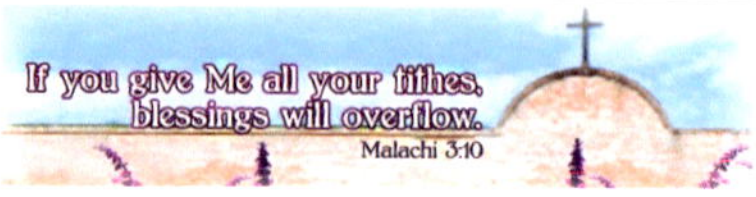

Monthly Financial Goals

What improvements can be made from last month? ____________________

Goals For This Month:

1. ____________________
2. ____________________
3. ____________________

To reach these goals I need to:

- [ ] ____________________
- [ ] ____________________
- [ ] ____________________
- [ ] ____________________
- [ ] ____________________
- [ ] ____________________
- [ ] ____________________
- [ ] ____________________

Notes:

BUDGET at a GLANCE

INCOME SOURCE	AMOUNT	PAYMENT DATE	COMMENTS
INCOME TOTALS			

EXPENSES	AMOUNT	DUE DATE	COMMENTS
Housing			
mortgage/rent			
second mortgage			
property taxes			
home insurance			
maintenance/repairs			
alarm system			
Utilities			
electricity			
heat			
water/sewer			
garbage pick-up			
home phone			
internet			
cable/satellite			
cell phones			
Food			
groceries			
meals out			

Monthly Financial Goals

What improvements can be made from last month? ______________________

Goals For This Month:

1. ______________________
2. ______________________
3. ______________________

To reach these goals I need to:

- [ ] ______________________
- [ ] ______________________
- [ ] ______________________
- [ ] ______________________
- [ ] ______________________
- [ ] ______________________
- [ ] ______________________
- [ ] ______________________

Notes:

BUDGET at a GLANCE

INCOME SOURCE	AMOUNT	PAYMENT DATE	COMMENTS
INCOME TOTALS			

EXPENSES	AMOUNT	DUE DATE	COMMENTS
Housing			
mortgage/rent			
second mortgage			
property taxes			
home insurance			
maintenance/repairs			
alarm system			
Utilities			
electricity			
heat			
water/sewer			
garbage pick-up			
home phone			
internet			
cable/satellite			
cell phones			
Food			
groceries			
meals out			

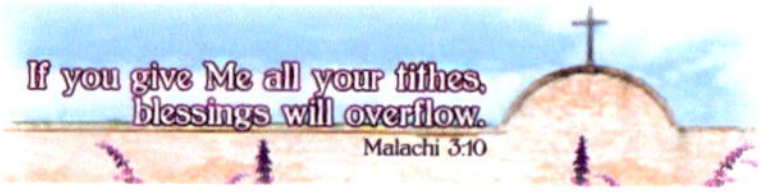

Monthly Financial Goals

What improvements can be made from last month? ______________________________

Goals For This Month:

1. ______________________________
2. ______________________________
3. ______________________________

To reach these goals I need to:

- [ ] ______________________________
- [ ] ______________________________
- [ ] ______________________________
- [ ] ______________________________
- [ ] ______________________________
- [ ] ______________________________
- [ ] ______________________________
- [ ] ______________________________

Notes:

BUDGET *at a* GLANCE

INCOME SOURCE	AMOUNT	PAYMENT DATE	COMMENTS
INCOME TOTALS			

EXPENSES	AMOUNT	DUE DATE	COMMENTS
Housing			
mortgage/rent			
second mortgage			
property taxes			
home insurance			
maintenance/repairs			
alarm system			
Utilities			
electricity			
heat			
water/sewer			
garbage pick-up			
home phone			
internet			
cable/satellite			
cell phones			
Food			
groceries			
meals out			

Monthly Financial Goals

What improvements can be made from last month? ______

Goals For This Month:

1. ______
2. ______
3. ______

To reach these goals I need to:

- [ ] ______
- [ ] ______
- [ ] ______
- [ ] ______
- [ ] ______
- [ ] ______
- [ ] ______
- [ ] ______

Notes:

BUDGET at a GLANCE

INCOME SOURCE	AMOUNT	PAYMENT DATE	COMMENTS
INCOME TOTALS			

EXPENSES	AMOUNT	DUE DATE	COMMENTS
Housing			
mortgage/rent			
second mortgage			
property taxes			
home insurance			
maintenance/repairs			
alarm system			
Utilities			
electricity			
heat			
water/sewer			
garbage pick-up			
home phone			
internet			
cable/satellite			
cell phones			
Food			
groceries			
meals out			

Monthly Financial Goals

What improvements can be made from last month? ____________________

Goals For This Month:

1. ____________________
2. ____________________
3. ____________________

To reach these goals I need to:

- [ ] ____________________
- [ ] ____________________
- [ ] ____________________
- [ ] ____________________
- [ ] ____________________
- [ ] ____________________
- [ ] ____________________
- [ ] ____________________

Notes:

BUDGET at a GLANCE

INCOME SOURCE	AMOUNT	PAYMENT DATE	COMMENTS
INCOME TOTALS			

EXPENSES	AMOUNT	DUE DATE	COMMENTS
Housing			
mortgage/rent			
second mortgage			
property taxes			
home insurance			
maintenance/repairs			
alarm system			
Utilities			
electricity			
heat			
water/sewer			
garbage pick-up			
home phone			
internet			
cable/satellite			
cell phones			
Food			
groceries			
meals out			

Monthly Financial Goals

What improvements can be made from last month? ______________________

Goals For This Month:

1. ______________________

2. ______________________

3. ______________________

To reach these goals I need to:

- [ ] ______________________
- [ ] ______________________
- [ ] ______________________
- [ ] ______________________
- [ ] ______________________
- [ ] ______________________
- [ ] ______________________
- [ ] ______________________

Notes:

BUDGET at a GLANCE

INCOME SOURCE	AMOUNT	PAYMENT DATE	COMMENTS
INCOME TOTALS			

EXPENSES	AMOUNT	DUE DATE	COMMENTS
Housing			
mortgage/rent			
second mortgage			
property taxes			
home insurance			
maintenance/repairs			
alarm system			
Utilities			
electricity			
heat			
water/sewer			
garbage pick-up			
home phone			
internet			
cable/satellite			
cell phones			
Food			
groceries			
meals out			

Monthly Financial Goals

What improvements can be made from last month? ___

Goals For This Month:

1. ___
2. ___
3. ___

To reach these goals I need to:

- [ ] ___
- [ ] ___
- [ ] ___
- [ ] ___
- [ ] ___
- [ ] ___
- [ ] ___
- [ ] ___

Notes:

BUDGET at a GLANCE

INCOME SOURCE	AMOUNT	PAYMENT DATE	COMMENTS
INCOME TOTALS			

EXPENSES	AMOUNT	DUE DATE	COMMENTS
Housing			
mortgage/rent			
second mortgage			
property taxes			
home insurance			
maintenance/repairs			
alarm system			
Utilities			
electricity			
heat			
water/sewer			
garbage pick-up			
home phone			
internet			
cable/satellite			
cell phones			
Food			
groceries			
meals out			

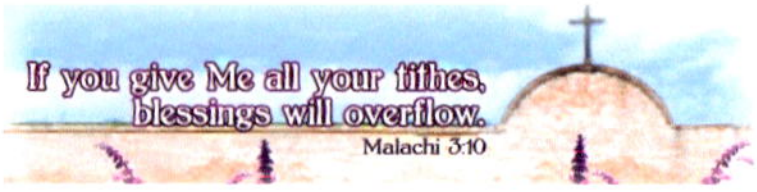

Monthly Financial Goals

What improvements can be made from last month? ______________________

Goals For This Month:

1. ______________________
2. ______________________
3. ______________________

To reach these goals I need to:

- [ ] ______________________
- [ ] ______________________
- [ ] ______________________
- [ ] ______________________
- [ ] ______________________
- [ ] ______________________
- [ ] ______________________
- [ ] ______________________

Notes:

BUDGET *at a* GLANCE

INCOME SOURCE	AMOUNT	PAYMENT DATE	COMMENTS
INCOME TOTALS			

EXPENSES	AMOUNT	DUE DATE	COMMENTS
Housing			
mortgage/rent			
second mortgage			
property taxes			
home insurance			
maintenance/repairs			
alarm system			
Utilities			
electricity			
heat			
water/sewer			
garbage pick-up			
home phone			
internet			
cable/satellite			
cell phones			
Food			
groceries			
meals out			

Monthly Financial Goals

What improvements can be made from last month? ____________________

Goals For This Month:

1. ____________________
2. ____________________
3. ____________________

To reach these goals I need to:

- [ ] ____________________
- [ ] ____________________
- [ ] ____________________
- [ ] ____________________
- [ ] ____________________
- [ ] ____________________
- [ ] ____________________
- [ ] ____________________

Notes:

BUDGET at a GLANCE

INCOME SOURCE	AMOUNT	PAYMENT DATE	COMMENTS
INCOME TOTALS			

EXPENSES	AMOUNT	DUE DATE	COMMENTS
Housing			
mortgage/rent			
second mortgage			
property taxes			
home insurance			
maintenance/repairs			
alarm system			
Utilities			
electricity			
heat			
water/sewer			
garbage pick-up			
home phone			
internet			
cable/satellite			
cell phones			
Food			
groceries			
meals out			

Monthly Financial Goals

What improvements can be made from last month? ____________________

Goals For This Month:

1. ____________________
2. ____________________
3. ____________________

To reach these goals I need to:

- [ ] ____________________
- [ ] ____________________
- [ ] ____________________
- [ ] ____________________
- [ ] ____________________
- [ ] ____________________
- [ ] ____________________
- [ ] ____________________

Notes:

BUDGET at a GLANCE

INCOME SOURCE	AMOUNT	PAYMENT DATE	COMMENTS
INCOME TOTALS			

EXPENSES	AMOUNT	DUE DATE	COMMENTS
Housing			
mortgage/rent			
second mortgage			
property taxes			
home insurance			
maintenance/repairs			
alarm system			
Utilities			
electricity			
heat			
water/sewer			
garbage pick-up			
home phone			
internet			
cable/satellite			
cell phones			
Food			
groceries			
meals out			

Monthly Financial Goals

What improvements can be made from last month? ____________________

Goals For This Month:

1. ____________________
2. ____________________
3. ____________________

To reach these goals I need to:

- [ ] ____________________
- [ ] ____________________
- [ ] ____________________
- [ ] ____________________
- [ ] ____________________
- [ ] ____________________
- [ ] ____________________
- [ ] ____________________

Notes:

BUDGET *at a* GLANCE

INCOME SOURCE	AMOUNT	PAYMENT DATE	COMMENTS
INCOME TOTALS			

EXPENSES	AMOUNT	DUE DATE	COMMENTS
Housing			
mortgage/rent			
second mortgage			
property taxes			
home insurance			
maintenance/repairs			
alarm system			
Utilities			
electricity			
heat			
water/sewer			
garbage pick-up			
home phone			
internet			
cable/satellite			
cell phones			
Food			
groceries			
meals out			

Monthly Financial Goals

What improvements can be made from last month? ____________________

Goals For This Month:

1. ____________________
2. ____________________
3. ____________________

To reach these goals I need to:

- [ ] ____________________
- [ ] ____________________
- [ ] ____________________
- [ ] ____________________
- [ ] ____________________
- [ ] ____________________
- [ ] ____________________
- [ ] ____________________

Notes:

BUDGET at a GLANCE

INCOME SOURCE	AMOUNT	PAYMENT DATE	COMMENTS
INCOME TOTALS			

EXPENSES	AMOUNT	DUE DATE	COMMENTS
Housing			
mortgage/rent			
second mortgage			
property taxes			
home insurance			
maintenance/repairs			
alarm system			
Utilities			
electricity			
heat			
water/sewer			
garbage pick-up			
home phone			
internet			
cable/satellite			
cell phones			
Food			
groceries			
meals out			

Monthly Financial Goals

What improvements can be made from last month? ____________________

Goals For This Month:

1. ____________________
2. ____________________
3. ____________________

To reach these goals I need to:

- [ ] ____________________
- [ ] ____________________
- [ ] ____________________
- [ ] ____________________
- [ ] ____________________
- [ ] ____________________
- [ ] ____________________
- [ ] ____________________

Notes:

BUDGET at a GLANCE

INCOME SOURCE	AMOUNT	PAYMENT DATE	COMMENTS
INCOME TOTALS			

EXPENSES	AMOUNT	DUE DATE	COMMENTS
Housing			
mortgage/rent			
second mortgage			
property taxes			
home insurance			
maintenance/repairs			
alarm system			
Utilities			
electricity			
heat			
water/sewer			
garbage pick-up			
home phone			
internet			
cable/satellite			
cell phones			
Food			
groceries			
meals out			

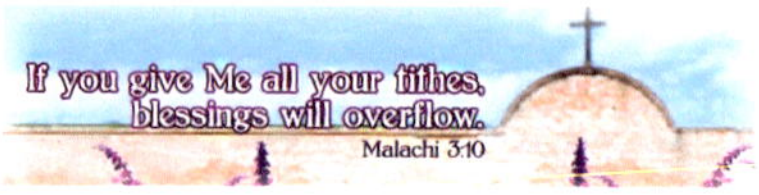

Monthly Financial Goals

What improvements can be made from last month? ____________________

Goals For This Month:

1. ____________________
2. ____________________
3. ____________________

To reach these goals I need to:

- [ ] ____________________
- [ ] ____________________
- [ ] ____________________
- [ ] ____________________
- [ ] ____________________
- [ ] ____________________
- [ ] ____________________
- [ ] ____________________

Notes:

BUDGET at a GLANCE

INCOME SOURCE	AMOUNT	PAYMENT DATE	COMMENTS
INCOME TOTALS			

EXPENSES	AMOUNT	DUE DATE	COMMENTS
Housing			
mortgage/rent			
second mortgage			
property taxes			
home insurance			
maintenance/repairs			
alarm system			
Utilities			
electricity			
heat			
water/sewer			
garbage pick-up			
home phone			
internet			
cable/satellite			
cell phones			
Food			
groceries			
meals out			

Monthly Financial Goals

What improvements can be made from last month? ____________________

Goals For This Month:

1. ____________________
2. ____________________
3. ____________________

To reach these goals I need to:

- ☐ ____________________
- ☐ ____________________
- ☐ ____________________
- ☐ ____________________
- ☐ ____________________
- ☐ ____________________
- ☐ ____________________
- ☐ ____________________

Notes:

BUDGET at a GLANCE

INCOME SOURCE	AMOUNT	PAYMENT DATE	COMMENTS
INCOME TOTALS			

EXPENSES	AMOUNT	DUE DATE	COMMENTS
Housing			
mortgage/rent			
second mortgage			
property taxes			
home insurance			
maintenance/repairs			
alarm system			
Utilities			
electricity			
heat			
water/sewer			
garbage pickup			
home phone			
internet			
cable/satellite			
cell phones			
Food			
groceries			
meals out			

Monthly Financial Goals

What improvements can be made from last month? ____________________

Goals For This Month:

1. ____________________
2. ____________________
3. ____________________

To reach these goals I need to:

- [ ] ____________________
- [ ] ____________________
- [ ] ____________________
- [ ] ____________________
- [ ] ____________________
- [ ] ____________________
- [ ] ____________________
- [ ] ____________________

Notes:

BUDGET at a GLANCE

INCOME SOURCE	AMOUNT	PAYMENT DATE	COMMENTS
INCOME TOTALS			

EXPENSES	AMOUNT	DUE DATE	COMMENTS
Housing			
mortgage/rent			
second mortgage			
property taxes			
home insurance			
maintenance/repairs			
alarm system			
Utilities			
electricity			
heat			
water/sewer			
garbage pick-up			
home phone			
internet			
cable/satellite			
cell phones			
Food			
groceries			
meals out			

Monthly Financial Goals

What improvements can be made from last month? ____________________

Goals For This Month:

1. ____________________
2. ____________________
3. ____________________

To reach these goals I need to:

- ☐ ____________________
- ☐ ____________________
- ☐ ____________________
- ☐ ____________________
- ☐ ____________________
- ☐ ____________________
- ☐ ____________________
- ☐ ____________________

Notes:

BUDGET at a GLANCE

INCOME SOURCE	AMOUNT	PAYMENT DATE	COMMENTS
INCOME TOTALS			

EXPENSES	AMOUNT	DUE DATE	COMMENTS
Housing			
mortgage/rent			
second mortgage			
property taxes			
home insurance			
maintenance/repairs			
alarm system			
Utilities			
electricity			
heat			
water/sewer			
garbage pick-up			
home phone			
internet			
cable/satellite			
cell phones			
Food			
groceries			
meals out			

Monthly Financial Goals

What improvements can be made from last month? ____________________

Goals For This Month:

1. ____________________
2. ____________________
3. ____________________

To reach these goals I need to:

- [ ] ____________________
- [ ] ____________________
- [ ] ____________________
- [ ] ____________________
- [ ] ____________________
- [ ] ____________________
- [ ] ____________________
- [ ] ____________________

Notes:

BUDGET at a GLANCE

INCOME SOURCE	AMOUNT	PAYMENT DATE	COMMENTS
INCOME TOTALS			

EXPENSES	AMOUNT	DUE DATE	COMMENTS
Housing			
mortgage/rent			
second mortgage			
property taxes			
home insurance			
maintenance/repairs			
alarm system			
Utilities			
electricity			
heat			
water/sewer			
garbage pick-up			
home phone			
internet			
cable/satellite			
cell phones			
Food			
groceries			
meals out			

Monthly Financial Goals

What improvements can be made from last month? ____________________

Goals For This Month:

1. ____________________

2. ____________________

3. ____________________

To reach these goals I need to:

- [ ] ____________________
- [ ] ____________________
- [ ] ____________________
- [ ] ____________________
- [ ] ____________________
- [ ] ____________________
- [ ] ____________________
- [ ] ____________________

Notes:

BUDGET *at a* GLANCE

INCOME SOURCE	AMOUNT	PAYMENT DATE	COMMENTS
INCOME TOTALS			

EXPENSES	AMOUNT	DUE DATE	COMMENTS
Housing			
mortgage/rent			
second mortgage			
property taxes			
home insurance			
maintenance/repairs			
alarm system			
Utilities			
electricity			
heat			
water/sewer			
garbage pick-up			
home phone			
internet			
cable/satellite			
cell phones			
Food			
groceries			
meals out			

Monthly Financial Goals

What improvements can be made from last month? ____________________

Goals For This Month:

1. ____________________

2. ____________________

3. ____________________

To reach these goals I need to:

- [ ] ____________________
- [ ] ____________________
- [ ] ____________________
- [ ] ____________________
- [ ] ____________________
- [ ] ____________________
- [ ] ____________________
- [ ] ____________________

Notes:

BUDGET at a GLANCE

INCOME SOURCE	AMOUNT	PAYMENT DATE	COMMENTS
INCOME TOTALS			

EXPENSES	AMOUNT	DUE DATE	COMMENTS
Housing			
mortgage/rent			
second mortgage			
property taxes			
home insurance			
maintenance/repairs			
alarm system			
Utilities			
electricity			
heat			
water/sewer			
garbage pick-up			
home phone			
internet			
cable/satellite			
cell phones			
Food			
groceries			
meals out			

Monthly Financial Goals

What improvements can be made from last month? ______________________

Goals For This Month:

1. ______________________
2. ______________________
3. ______________________

To reach these goals I need to:

- [ ] ______________________
- [ ] ______________________
- [ ] ______________________
- [ ] ______________________
- [ ] ______________________
- [ ] ______________________
- [ ] ______________________
- [ ] ______________________

Notes:

BUDGET at a GLANCE

INCOME SOURCE	AMOUNT	PAYMENT DATE	COMMENTS
INCOME TOTALS			

EXPENSES	AMOUNT	DUE DATE	COMMENTS
Housing			
mortgage/rent			
second mortgage			
property taxes			
home insurance			
maintenance/repairs			
alarm system			
Utilities			
electricity			
heat			
water/sewer			
garbage pick-up			
home phone			
internet			
cable/satellite			
cell phones			
Food			
groceries			
meals out			

Monthly Financial Goals

What improvements can be made from last month? ____________________

Goals For This Month:

1. ____________________
2. ____________________
3. ____________________

To reach these goals I need to:

- ☐ ____________________
- ☐ ____________________
- ☐ ____________________
- ☐ ____________________
- ☐ ____________________
- ☐ ____________________
- ☐ ____________________
- ☐ ____________________

Notes:

BUDGET at a GLANCE

INCOME SOURCE	AMOUNT	PAYMENT DATE	COMMENTS
INCOME TOTALS			

EXPENSES	AMOUNT	DUE DATE	COMMENTS
Housing			
mortgage/rent			
second mortgage			
property taxes			
home insurance			
maintenance/repairs			
alarm system			
Utilities			
electricity			
heat			
water/sewer			
garbage pick-up			
home phone			
internet			
cable/satellite			
cell phones			
Food			
groceries			
meals out			

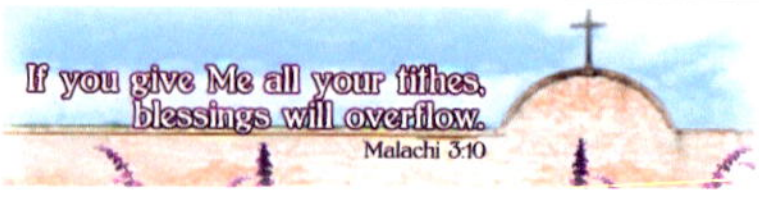

Monthly Financial Goals

What improvements can be made from last month? ____________________

Goals For This Month:

1. ____________________
2. ____________________
3. ____________________

To reach these goals I need to:

- [ ] ____________________
- [ ] ____________________
- [ ] ____________________
- [ ] ____________________
- [ ] ____________________
- [ ] ____________________
- [ ] ____________________
- [ ] ____________________

Notes:

BUDGET at a GLANCE

INCOME SOURCE	AMOUNT	PAYMENT DATE	COMMENTS
INCOME TOTALS			

EXPENSES	AMOUNT	DUE DATE	COMMENTS
Housing			
mortgage/rent			
second mortgage			
property taxes			
home insurance			
maintenance/repairs			
alarm system			
Utilities			
electricity			
heat			
water/sewer			
garbage pick-up			
home phone			
internet			
cable/satellite			
cell phones			
Food			
groceries			
meals out			

Monthly Financial Goals

What improvements can be made from last month? ____________________

Goals For This Month:

1. ____________________
2. ____________________
3. ____________________

To reach these goals I need to:

- [ ] ____________________
- [ ] ____________________
- [ ] ____________________
- [ ] ____________________
- [ ] ____________________
- [ ] ____________________
- [ ] ____________________
- [ ] ____________________

Notes:

BUDGET at a GLANCE

INCOME SOURCE	AMOUNT	PAYMENT DATE	COMMENTS
INCOME TOTALS			

EXPENSES	AMOUNT	DUE DATE	COMMENTS
Housing			
mortgage/rent			
second mortgage			
property taxes			
home insurance			
maintenance/repairs			
alarm system			
Utilities			
electricity			
heat			
water/sewer			
garbage pick-up			
home phone			
internet			
cable/satellite			
cell phones			
Food			
groceries			
meals out			

Monthly Financial Goals

What improvements can be made from last month? ______________________

Goals For This Month:

1. ______________________
2. ______________________
3. ______________________

To reach these goals I need to:

- [ ] ______________________
- [ ] ______________________
- [ ] ______________________
- [ ] ______________________
- [ ] ______________________
- [ ] ______________________
- [ ] ______________________
- [ ] ______________________

Notes:

BUDGET at a GLANCE

INCOME SOURCE	AMOUNT	PAYMENT DATE	COMMENTS
INCOME TOTALS			

EXPENSES	AMOUNT	DUE DATE	COMMENTS
Housing			
mortgage/rent			
second mortgage			
property taxes			
home insurance			
maintenance/repairs			
alarm system			
Utilities			
electricity			
heat			
water/sewer			
garbage pick-up			
home phone			
internet			
cable/satellite			
cell phones			
Food			
groceries			
meals out			

Monthly Financial Goals

What improvements can be made from last month? ______________________________

Goals For This Month:

1. ______________________________
2. ______________________________
3. ______________________________

To reach these goals I need to:

- [ ] ______________________________
- [ ] ______________________________
- [ ] ______________________________
- [ ] ______________________________
- [ ] ______________________________
- [ ] ______________________________
- [ ] ______________________________
- [ ] ______________________________

Notes:

BUDGET at a GLANCE

INCOME SOURCE	AMOUNT	PAYMENT DATE	COMMENTS
INCOME TOTALS			

EXPENSES	AMOUNT	DUE DATE	COMMENTS
Housing			
mortgage/rent			
second mortgage			
property taxes			
home insurance			
maintenance/repairs			
alarm system			
Utilities			
electricity			
heat			
water/sewer			
garbage pick-up			
home phone			
internet			
cable/satellite			
cell phones			
Food			
groceries			
meals out			

Monthly Financial Goals

What improvements can be made from last month? ____________________

Goals For This Month:

1. ____________________
2. ____________________
3. ____________________

To reach these goals I need to:

- [ ] ____________________
- [ ] ____________________
- [ ] ____________________
- [ ] ____________________
- [ ] ____________________
- [ ] ____________________
- [ ] ____________________
- [ ] ____________________

Notes:

BUDGET at a GLANCE

INCOME SOURCE	AMOUNT	PAYMENT DATE	COMMENTS
INCOME TOTALS			

EXPENSES	AMOUNT	DUE DATE	COMMENTS
Housing			
mortgage/rent			
second mortgage			
property taxes			
home insurance			
maintenance/repairs			
alarm system			
Utilities			
electricity			
heat			
water/sewer			
garbage pick-up			
home phone			
internet			
cable/satellite			
cell phones			
Food			
groceries			
meals out			

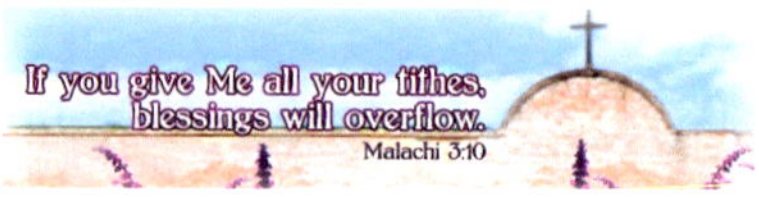

Monthly Financial Goals

What improvements can be made from last month? ______________________________

Goals For This Month:

1. ______________________________
2. ______________________________
3. ______________________________

To reach these goals I need to:

- [ ] ______________________________
- [ ] ______________________________
- [ ] ______________________________
- [ ] ______________________________
- [ ] ______________________________
- [ ] ______________________________
- [ ] ______________________________
- [ ] ______________________________

Notes:

BUDGET at a GLANCE

INCOME SOURCE	AMOUNT	PAYMENT DATE	COMMENTS
INCOME TOTALS			

EXPENSES	AMOUNT	DUE DATE	COMMENTS
Housing			
mortgage/rent			
second mortgage			
property taxes			
home insurance			
maintenance/repairs			
alarm system			
Utilities			
electricity			
heat			
water/sewer			
garbage pick-up			
home phone			
internet			
cable/satellite			
cell phones			
Food			
groceries			
meals out			

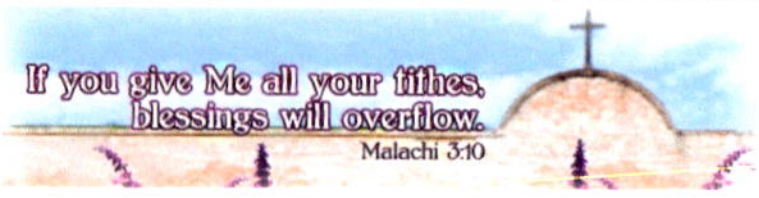

Monthly Financial Goals

What improvements can be made from last month? ____________________

Goals For This Month:

1. ____________________
2. ____________________
3. ____________________

To reach these goals I need to:

- [ ] ____________________
- [ ] ____________________
- [ ] ____________________
- [ ] ____________________
- [ ] ____________________
- [ ] ____________________
- [ ] ____________________
- [ ] ____________________

Notes:

BUDGET at a GLANCE

INCOME SOURCE	AMOUNT	PAYMENT DATE	COMMENTS
INCOME TOTALS			

EXPENSES	AMOUNT	DUE DATE	COMMENTS
Housing			
mortgage/rent			
second mortgage			
property taxes			
home insurance			
maintenance/repairs			
alarm system			
Utilities			
electricity			
heat			
water/sewer			
garbage pick-up			
home phone			
internet			
cable/satellite			
cell phones			
Food			
groceries			
meals out			

Monthly Financial Goals

What improvements can be made from last month? ____________________

Goals For This Month:

1. ____________________
2. ____________________
3. ____________________

To reach these goals I need to:

- ☐ ____________________
- ☐ ____________________
- ☐ ____________________
- ☐ ____________________
- ☐ ____________________
- ☐ ____________________
- ☐ ____________________
- ☐ ____________________

Notes:

BUDGET *at a* GLANCE

INCOME SOURCE	AMOUNT	PAYMENT DATE	COMMENTS
INCOME TOTALS			

EXPENSES	AMOUNT	DUE DATE	COMMENTS
Housing			
mortgage/rent			
second mortgage			
property taxes			
home insurance			
maintenance/repairs			
alarm system			
Utilities			
electricity			
heat			
water/sewer			
garbage pick-up			
home phone			
internet			
cable/satellite			
cell phones			
Food			
groceries			
meals out			

Monthly Financial Goals

What improvements can be made from last month? ____________________

Goals For This Month:

1. ____________________
2. ____________________
3. ____________________

To reach these goals I need to:

- [ ] ____________________
- [ ] ____________________
- [ ] ____________________
- [ ] ____________________
- [ ] ____________________
- [ ] ____________________
- [ ] ____________________
- [ ] ____________________

Notes:

BUDGET *at a* GLANCE

INCOME SOURCE	AMOUNT	PAYMENT DATE	COMMENTS
INCOME TOTALS			

EXPENSES	AMOUNT	DUE DATE	COMMENTS
Housing			
mortgage/rent			
second mortgage			
property taxes			
home insurance			
maintenance/repairs			
alarm system			
Utilities			
electricity			
heat			
water/sewer			
garbage pick-up			
home phone			
internet			
cable/satellite			
cell phones			
Food			
groceries			
meals out			

Monthly Financial Goals

What improvements can be made from last month? ______

Goals For This Month:

1. ______
2. ______
3. ______

To reach these goals I need to:

- [ ] ______
- [ ] ______
- [ ] ______
- [ ] ______
- [ ] ______
- [ ] ______
- [ ] ______
- [ ] ______

Notes:

BUDGET at a GLANCE

INCOME SOURCE	AMOUNT	PAYMENT DATE	COMMENTS
INCOME TOTALS			

EXPENSES	AMOUNT	DUE DATE	COMMENTS
Housing			
mortgage/rent			
second mortgage			
property taxes			
home insurance			
maintenance/repairs			
alarm system			
Utilities			
electricity			
heat			
water/sewer			
garbage pick-up			
home phone			
internet			
cable/satellite			
cell phones			
Food			
groceries			
meals out			

Monthly Financial Goals

What improvements can be made from last month? ______________________

Goals For This Month:

1. ______________________
2. ______________________
3. ______________________

To reach these goals I need to:

- [ ] ______________________
- [ ] ______________________
- [ ] ______________________
- [ ] ______________________
- [ ] ______________________
- [ ] ______________________
- [ ] ______________________
- [ ] ______________________

Notes:

BUDGET at a GLANCE

INCOME SOURCE	AMOUNT	PAYMENT DATE	COMMENTS
INCOME TOTALS			

EXPENSES	AMOUNT	DUE DATE	COMMENTS
Housing			
mortgage/rent			
second mortgage			
property taxes			
home insurance			
maintenance/repairs			
alarm system			
Utilities			
electricity			
heat			
water/sewer			
garbage pick-up			
home phone			
internet			
cable/satellite			
cell phones			
Food			
groceries			
meals out			

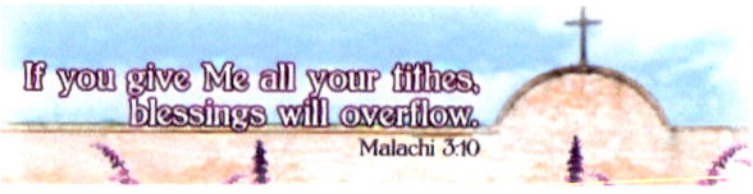

Monthly Financial Goals

What improvements can be made from last month? ______________________

Goals For This Month:

1. ______________________

2. ______________________

3. ______________________

To reach these goals I need to:

- ☐ ______________________
- ☐ ______________________
- ☐ ______________________
- ☐ ______________________
- ☐ ______________________
- ☐ ______________________
- ☐ ______________________
- ☐ ______________________

Notes:

BUDGET at a GLANCE

INCOME SOURCE	AMOUNT	PAYMENT DATE	COMMENTS
INCOME TOTALS			

EXPENSES	AMOUNT	DUE DATE	COMMENTS
Housing			
mortgage/rent			
second mortgage			
property taxes			
home insurance			
maintenance/repairs			
alarm system			
Utilities			
electricity			
heat			
water/sewer			
garbage pick-up			
home phone			
internet			
cable/satellite			
cell phones			
Food			
groceries			
meals out			

Monthly Financial Goals

What improvements can be made from last month? ____________________

Goals For This Month:

1. ____________________

2. ____________________

3. ____________________

To reach these goals I need to:

- [ ] ____________________
- [ ] ____________________
- [ ] ____________________
- [ ] ____________________
- [ ] ____________________
- [ ] ____________________
- [ ] ____________________
- [ ] ____________________

Notes:

BUDGET *at a* GLANCE

INCOME SOURCE	AMOUNT	PAYMENT DATE	COMMENTS
INCOME TOTALS			

EXPENSES	AMOUNT	DUE DATE	COMMENTS
Housing			
mortgage/rent			
second mortgage			
property taxes			
home insurance			
maintenance/repairs			
alarm system			
Utilities			
electricity			
heat			
water/sewer			
garbage pick-up			
home phone			
internet			
cable/satellite			
cell phones			
Food			
groceries			
meals out			

Monthly Financial Goals

What improvements can be made from last month? ____________________

Goals For This Month:

1. ____________________
2. ____________________
3. ____________________

To reach these goals I need to:

- [ ] ____________________
- [ ] ____________________
- [ ] ____________________
- [ ] ____________________
- [ ] ____________________
- [ ] ____________________
- [ ] ____________________
- [ ] ____________________

Notes:

BUDGET at a GLANCE

INCOME SOURCE	AMOUNT	PAYMENT DATE	COMMENTS
INCOME TOTALS			

EXPENSES	AMOUNT	DUE DATE	COMMENTS
Housing			
mortgage/rent			
second mortgage			
property taxes			
home insurance			
maintenance/repairs			
alarm system			
Utilities			
electricity			
heat			
water/sewer			
garbage pick-up			
home phone			
internet			
cable/satellite			
cell phones			
Food			
groceries			
meals out			

Monthly Financial Goals

What improvements can be made from last month? ____________________

Goals For This Month:

1. ____________________
2. ____________________
3. ____________________

To reach these goals I need to:

- [ ] ____________________
- [ ] ____________________
- [ ] ____________________
- [ ] ____________________
- [ ] ____________________
- [ ] ____________________
- [ ] ____________________
- [ ] ____________________

Notes:

BUDGET at a GLANCE

INCOME SOURCE	AMOUNT	PAYMENT DATE	COMMENTS
INCOME TOTALS			

EXPENSES	AMOUNT	DUE DATE	COMMENTS
Housing			
mortgage/rent			
second mortgage			
property taxes			
home insurance			
maintenance/repairs			
alarm system			
Utilities			
electricity			
heat			
water/sewer			
garbage pick-up			
home phone			
internet			
cable/satellite			
cell phones			
Food			
groceries			
meals out			

Monthly Financial Goals

What improvements can be made from last month? ______________________

Goals For This Month:

1. ______________________
2. ______________________
3. ______________________

To reach these goals I need to:

- [ ] ______________________
- [ ] ______________________
- [ ] ______________________
- [ ] ______________________
- [ ] ______________________
- [ ] ______________________
- [ ] ______________________
- [ ] ______________________

Notes:

BUDGET at a GLANCE

INCOME SOURCE	AMOUNT	PAYMENT DATE	COMMENTS
INCOME TOTALS			

EXPENSES	AMOUNT	DUE DATE	COMMENTS
Housing			
mortgage/rent			
second mortgage			
property taxes			
home insurance			
maintenance/repairs			
alarm system			
Utilities			
electricity			
heat			
water/sewer			
garbage pick-up			
home phone			
internet			
cable/satellite			
cell phones			
Food			
groceries			
meals out			

Monthly Financial Goals

What improvements can be made from last month? ____________________

Goals For This Month:

1. ____________________
2. ____________________
3. ____________________

To reach these goals I need to:

- [ ] ____________________
- [ ] ____________________
- [ ] ____________________
- [ ] ____________________
- [ ] ____________________
- [ ] ____________________
- [ ] ____________________
- [ ] ____________________

Notes:

BUDGET at a GLANCE

INCOME SOURCE	AMOUNT	PAYMENT DATE	COMMENTS
INCOME TOTALS			

EXPENSES	AMOUNT	DUE DATE	COMMENTS
Housing			
mortgage/rent			
second mortgage			
property taxes			
home insurance			
maintenance/repairs			
alarm system			
Utilities			
electricity			
heat			
water/sewer			
garbage pick-up			
home phone			
internet			
cable/satellite			
cell phones			
Food			
groceries			
meals out			

Monthly Financial Goals

What improvements can be made from last month? ____________________

Goals For This Month:

1. ____________________
2. ____________________
3. ____________________

To reach these goals I need to:

- [ ] ____________________
- [ ] ____________________
- [ ] ____________________
- [ ] ____________________
- [ ] ____________________
- [ ] ____________________
- [ ] ____________________
- [ ] ____________________

Notes:

BUDGET at a GLANCE

INCOME SOURCE	AMOUNT	PAYMENT DATE	COMMENTS
INCOME TOTALS			

EXPENSES	AMOUNT	DUE DATE	COMMENTS
Housing			
mortgage/rent			
second mortgage			
property taxes			
home insurance			
maintenance/repairs			
alarm system			
Utilities			
electricity			
heat			
water/sewer			
garbage pick-up			
home phone			
internet			
cable/satellite			
cell phones			
Food			
groceries			
meals out			

Monthly Financial Goals

What improvements can be made from last month? ______________________________

Goals For This Month:

1. ______________________________
2. ______________________________
3. ______________________________

To reach these goals I need to:

- [ ] ______________________________
- [ ] ______________________________
- [ ] ______________________________
- [ ] ______________________________
- [ ] ______________________________
- [ ] ______________________________
- [ ] ______________________________
- [ ] ______________________________

Notes:

BUDGET at a GLANCE

INCOME SOURCE	AMOUNT	PAYMENT DATE	COMMENTS
INCOME TOTALS			

EXPENSES	AMOUNT	DUE DATE	COMMENTS
Housing			
mortgage/rent			
second mortgage			
property taxes			
home insurance			
maintenance/repairs			
alarm system			
Utilities			
electricity			
heat			
water/sewer			
garbage pick-up			
home phone			
internet			
cable/satellite			
cell phones			
Food			
groceries			
meals out			

Monthly Financial Goals

What improvements can be made from last month? ____________________

Goals For This Month:

1. ____________________
2. ____________________
3. ____________________

To reach these goals I need to:

- [ ] ____________________
- [ ] ____________________
- [ ] ____________________
- [ ] ____________________
- [ ] ____________________
- [ ] ____________________
- [ ] ____________________
- [ ] ____________________

Notes:

BUDGET at a GLANCE

INCOME SOURCE	AMOUNT	PAYMENT DATE	COMMENTS
INCOME TOTALS			

EXPENSES	AMOUNT	DUE DATE	COMMENTS
Housing			
mortgage/rent			
second mortgage			
property taxes			
home insurance			
maintenance/repairs			
alarm system			
Utilities			
electricity			
heat			
water/sewer			
garbage pick-up			
home phone			
internet			
cable/satellite			
cell phones			
Food			
groceries			
meals out			

Monthly Financial Goals

What improvements can be made from last month? ______________________________

Goals For This Month:

1. ______________________________

2. ______________________________

3. ______________________________

To reach these goals I need to:

- [ ] ______________________________
- [ ] ______________________________
- [ ] ______________________________
- [ ] ______________________________
- [ ] ______________________________
- [ ] ______________________________
- [ ] ______________________________
- [ ] ______________________________

Notes:

BUDGET at a GLANCE

INCOME SOURCE	AMOUNT	PAYMENT DATE	COMMENTS
INCOME TOTALS			

EXPENSES	AMOUNT	DUE DATE	COMMENTS
Housing			
mortgage/rent			
second mortgage			
property taxes			
home insurance			
maintenance/repairs			
alarm system			
Utilities			
electricity			
heat			
water/sewer			
garbage pick-up			
home phone			
internet			
cable/satellite			
cell phones			
Food			
groceries			
meals out			

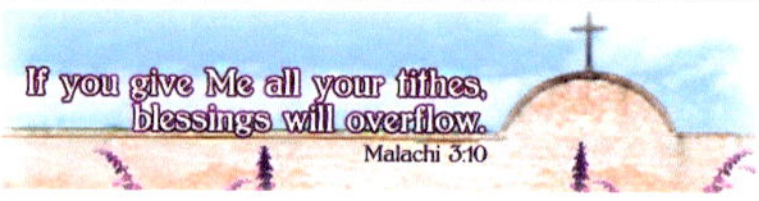

Monthly Financial Goals

What improvements can be made from last month? ______

Goals For This Month:

1. ______
2. ______
3. ______

To reach these goals I need to:

- ☐ ______
- ☐ ______
- ☐ ______
- ☐ ______
- ☐ ______
- ☐ ______
- ☐ ______
- ☐ ______

Notes:

BUDGET *at a* GLANCE

INCOME SOURCE	AMOUNT	PAYMENT DATE	COMMENTS
INCOME TOTALS			

EXPENSES	AMOUNT	DUE DATE	COMMENTS
Housing			
mortgage/rent			
second mortgage			
property taxes			
home insurance			
maintenance/repairs			
alarm system			
Utilities			
electricity			
heat			
water/sewer			
garbage pick-up			
home phone			
internet			
cable/satellite			
cell phones			
Food			
groceries			
meals out			

Monthly Financial Goals

What improvements can be made from last month? ____________________

Goals For This Month:

1. ____________________
2. ____________________
3. ____________________

To reach these goals I need to:

- [ ] ____________________
- [ ] ____________________
- [ ] ____________________
- [ ] ____________________
- [ ] ____________________
- [ ] ____________________
- [ ] ____________________
- [ ] ____________________

Notes:

BUDGET at a GLANCE

INCOME SOURCE	AMOUNT	PAYMENT DATE	COMMENTS
INCOME TOTALS			

EXPENSES	AMOUNT	DUE DATE	COMMENTS
Housing			
mortgage/rent			
second mortgage			
property taxes			
home insurance			
maintenance/repairs			
alarm system			
Utilities			
electricity			
heat			
water/sewer			
garbage pick-up			
home phone			
internet			
cable/satellite			
cell phones			
Food			
groceries			
meals out			

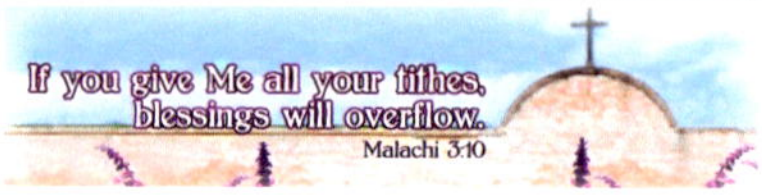

Monthly Financial Goals

What improvements can be made from last month? ______________________

Goals For This Month:

1. ______________________

2. ______________________

3. ______________________

To reach these goals I need to:

- [ ] ______________________
- [ ] ______________________
- [ ] ______________________
- [ ] ______________________
- [ ] ______________________
- [ ] ______________________
- [ ] ______________________
- [ ] ______________________

Notes:

BUDGET at a GLANCE

INCOME SOURCE	AMOUNT	PAYMENT DATE	COMMENTS
INCOME TOTALS			

EXPENSES	AMOUNT	DUE DATE	COMMENTS
Housing			
mortgage/rent			
second mortgage			
property taxes			
home insurance			
maintenance/repairs			
alarm system			
Utilities			
electricity			
heat			
water/sewer			
garbage pick-up			
home phone			
internet			
cable/satellite			
cell phones			
Food			
groceries			
meals out			

Monthly Financial Goals

What improvements can be made from last month? ______________________

Goals For This Month:

1. ______________________

2. ______________________

3. ______________________

To reach these goals I need to:

- [ ] ______________________
- [ ] ______________________
- [ ] ______________________
- [ ] ______________________
- [ ] ______________________
- [ ] ______________________
- [ ] ______________________
- [ ] ______________________

Notes:

BUDGET at a GLANCE

INCOME SOURCE	AMOUNT	PAYMENT DATE	COMMENTS
INCOME TOTALS			

EXPENSES	AMOUNT	DUE DATE	COMMENTS
Housing			
mortgage/rent			
second mortgage			
property taxes			
home insurance			
maintenance/repairs			
alarm system			
Utilities			
electricity			
heat			
water/sewer			
garbage pick-up			
home phone			
internet			
cable/satellite			
cell phones			
Food			
groceries			
meals out			

Monthly Financial Goals

What improvements can be made from last month? ____________________

Goals For This Month:

1. ____________________
2. ____________________
3. ____________________

To reach these goals I need to:

- [ ] ____________________
- [ ] ____________________
- [ ] ____________________
- [ ] ____________________
- [ ] ____________________
- [ ] ____________________
- [ ] ____________________
- [ ] ____________________

Notes:

BUDGET *at a* GLANCE

INCOME SOURCE	AMOUNT	PAYMENT DATE	COMMENTS
INCOME TOTALS			

EXPENSES	AMOUNT	DUE DATE	COMMENTS
Housing			
mortgage/rent			
second mortgage			
property taxes			
home insurance			
maintenance/repairs			
alarm system			
Utilities			
electricity			
heat			
water/sewer			
garbage pick-up			
home phone			
internet			
cable/satellite			
cell phones			
Food			
groceries			
meals out			

Monthly Financial Goals

What improvements can be made from last month? ________________

Goals For This Month:

1. ________________
2. ________________
3. ________________

To reach these goals I need to:

- [ ] ________________
- [ ] ________________
- [ ] ________________
- [ ] ________________
- [ ] ________________
- [ ] ________________
- [ ] ________________
- [ ] ________________

Notes:

BUDGET *at a* GLANCE

INCOME SOURCE	AMOUNT	PAYMENT DATE	COMMENTS
INCOME TOTALS			

EXPENSES	AMOUNT	DUE DATE	COMMENTS
Housing			
mortgage/rent			
second mortgage			
property taxes			
home insurance			
maintenance/repairs			
alarm system			
Utilities			
electricity			
heat			
water/sewer			
garbage pick-up			
home phone			
internet			
cable/satellite			
cell phones			
Food			
groceries			
meals out			

Monthly Financial Goals

What improvements can be made from last month? ______________________________

Goals For This Month:

1. ______________________________

2. ______________________________

3. ______________________________

To reach these goals I need to:

- [ ] ______________________________
- [ ] ______________________________
- [ ] ______________________________
- [ ] ______________________________
- [ ] ______________________________
- [ ] ______________________________
- [ ] ______________________________
- [ ] ______________________________

Notes:

BUDGET at a GLANCE

INCOME SOURCE	AMOUNT	PAYMENT DATE	COMMENTS
INCOME TOTALS			

EXPENSES	AMOUNT	DUE DATE	COMMENTS
Housing			
mortgage/rent			
second mortgage			
property taxes			
home insurance			
maintenance/repairs			
alarm system			
Utilities			
electricity			
heat			
water/sewer			
garbage pick-up			
home phone			
internet			
cable/satellite			
cell phones			
Food			
groceries			
meals out			

Monthly Financial Goals

What improvements can be made from last month? ____________________________

Goals For This Month:

1. ____________________________
2. ____________________________
3. ____________________________

To reach these goals I need to:

- [ ] ____________________________
- [ ] ____________________________
- [ ] ____________________________
- [ ] ____________________________
- [ ] ____________________________
- [ ] ____________________________
- [ ] ____________________________
- [ ] ____________________________

Notes:

BUDGET at a GLANCE

INCOME SOURCE	AMOUNT	PAYMENT DATE	COMMENTS
INCOME TOTALS			

EXPENSES	AMOUNT	DUE DATE	COMMENTS
Housing			
mortgage/rent			
second mortgage			
property taxes			
home insurance			
maintenance/repairs			
alarm system			
Utilities			
electricity			
heat			
water/sewer			
garbage pick-up			
home phone			
internet			
cable/satellite			
cell phones			
Food			
groceries			
meals out			

Monthly Financial Goals

What improvements can be made from last month? ______________________

Goals For This Month:

1. ______________________
2. ______________________
3. ______________________

To reach these goals I need to:

- [ ] ______________________
- [ ] ______________________
- [ ] ______________________
- [ ] ______________________
- [ ] ______________________
- [ ] ______________________
- [ ] ______________________
- [ ] ______________________

Notes:

BUDGET *at a* GLANCE

INCOME SOURCE	AMOUNT	PAYMENT DATE	COMMENTS
INCOME TOTALS			

EXPENSES	AMOUNT	DUE DATE	COMMENTS
Housing			
mortgage/rent			
second mortgage			
property taxes			
home insurance			
maintenance/repairs			
alarm system			
Utilities			
electricity			
heat			
water/sewer			
garbage pick-up			
home phone			
internet			
cable/satellite			
cell phones			
Food			
groceries			
meals out			

Monthly Financial Goals

What improvements can be made from last month? ____________________

Goals For This Month:

1. ____________________
2. ____________________
3. ____________________

To reach these goals I need to:

- ☐ ____________________
- ☐ ____________________
- ☐ ____________________
- ☐ ____________________
- ☐ ____________________
- ☐ ____________________
- ☐ ____________________
- ☐ ____________________

Notes:

BUDGET *at a* GLANCE

INCOME SOURCE	AMOUNT	PAYMENT DATE	COMMENTS
INCOME TOTALS			

EXPENSES	AMOUNT	DUE DATE	COMMENTS
Housing			
mortgage/rent			
second mortgage			
property taxes			
home insurance			
maintenance/repairs			
alarm system			
Utilities			
electricity			
heat			
water/sewer			
garbage pick-up			
home phone			
internet			
cable/satellite			
cell phones			
Food			
groceries			
meals out			

Monthly Financial Goals

What improvements can be made from last month? ____________________

Goals For This Month:

1. ____________________

2. ____________________

3. ____________________

To reach these goals I need to:

- [ ] ____________________
- [ ] ____________________
- [ ] ____________________
- [ ] ____________________
- [ ] ____________________
- [ ] ____________________
- [ ] ____________________
- [ ] ____________________

Notes:

BUDGET at a GLANCE

INCOME SOURCE	AMOUNT	PAYMENT DATE	COMMENTS
INCOME TOTALS			

EXPENSES	AMOUNT	DUE DATE	COMMENTS
Housing			
mortgage/rent			
second mortgage			
property taxes			
home insurance			
maintenance/repairs			
alarm system			
Utilities			
electricity			
heat			
water/sewer			
garbage pick-up			
home phone			
internet			
cable/satellite			
cell phones			
Food			
groceries			
meals out			

Monthly Financial Goals

What improvements can be made from last month? ____________________

Goals For This Month:

1. ____________________

2. ____________________

3. ____________________

To reach these goals I need to:

- [ ] ____________________
- [ ] ____________________
- [ ] ____________________
- [ ] ____________________
- [ ] ____________________
- [ ] ____________________
- [ ] ____________________
- [ ] ____________________

Notes:

BUDGET at a GLANCE

INCOME SOURCE	AMOUNT	PAYMENT DATE	COMMENTS
INCOME TOTALS			

EXPENSES	AMOUNT	DUE DATE	COMMENTS
Housing			
mortgage/rent			
second mortgage			
property taxes			
home insurance			
maintenance/repairs			
alarm system			
Utilities			
electricity			
heat			
water/sewer			
garbage pick-up			
home phone			
internet			
cable/satellite			
cell phones			
Food			
groceries			
meals out			

Monthly Financial Goals

What improvements can be made from last month? ______________________

Goals For This Month:

1. ______________________

2. ______________________

3. ______________________

To reach these goals I need to:

- [ ] ______________________
- [ ] ______________________
- [ ] ______________________
- [ ] ______________________
- [ ] ______________________
- [ ] ______________________
- [ ] ______________________
- [ ] ______________________

Notes:

BUDGET at a GLANCE

INCOME SOURCE	AMOUNT	PAYMENT DATE	COMMENTS
INCOME TOTALS			

EXPENSES	AMOUNT	DUE DATE	COMMENTS
Housing			
mortgage/rent			
second mortgage			
property taxes			
home insurance			
maintenance/repairs			
alarm system			
Utilities			
electricity			
heat			
water/sewer			
garbage pick-up			
home phone			
internet			
cable/satellite			
cell phones			
Food			
groceries			
meals out			

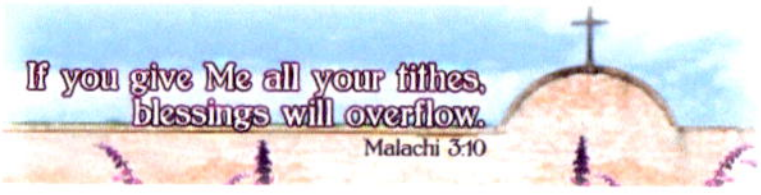

Monthly Financial Goals

What improvements can be made from last month? ______________________

Goals For This Month:

1. ______________________

2. ______________________

3. ______________________

To reach these goals I need to:

- [ ] ______________________
- [ ] ______________________
- [ ] ______________________
- [ ] ______________________
- [ ] ______________________
- [ ] ______________________
- [ ] ______________________
- [ ] ______________________

Notes:

BUDGET at a GLANCE

INCOME SOURCE	AMOUNT	PAYMENT DATE	COMMENTS
INCOME TOTALS			

EXPENSES	AMOUNT	DUE DATE	COMMENTS
Housing			
mortgage/rent			
second mortgage			
property taxes			
home insurance			
maintenance/repairs			
alarm system			
Utilities			
electricity			
heat			
water/sewer			
garbage pick-up			
home phone			
internet			
cable/satellite			
cell phones			
Food			
groceries			
meals out			

Monthly Financial Goals

What improvements can be made from last month? ______________________

Goals For This Month:

1. ______________________

2. ______________________

3. ______________________

To reach these goals I need to:

- [ ] ______________________
- [ ] ______________________
- [ ] ______________________
- [ ] ______________________
- [ ] ______________________
- [ ] ______________________
- [ ] ______________________
- [ ] ______________________

Notes:

BUDGET at a GLANCE

INCOME SOURCE	AMOUNT	PAYMENT DATE	COMMENTS
INCOME TOTALS			

EXPENSES	AMOUNT	DUE DATE	COMMENTS
Housing			
mortgage/rent			
second mortgage			
property taxes			
home insurance			
maintenance/repairs			
alarm system			
Utilities			
electricity			
heat			
water/sewer			
garbage pick-up			
home phone			
internet			
cable/satellite			
cell phones			
Food			
groceries			
meals out			

Monthly Financial Goals

What improvements can be made from last month? ____________________

Goals For This Month:

1. ____________________
2. ____________________
3. ____________________

To reach these goals I need to:

- [ ] ____________________
- [ ] ____________________
- [ ] ____________________
- [ ] ____________________
- [ ] ____________________
- [ ] ____________________
- [ ] ____________________
- [ ] ____________________

Notes:

BUDGET at a GLANCE

INCOME SOURCE	AMOUNT	PAYMENT DATE	COMMENTS
INCOME TOTALS			

EXPENSES	AMOUNT	DUE DATE	COMMENTS
Housing			
mortgage/rent			
second mortgage			
property taxes			
home insurance			
maintenance/repairs			
alarm system			
Utilities			
electricity			
heat			
water/sewer			
garbage pick-up			
home phone			
internet			
cable/satellite			
cell phones			
Food			
groceries			
meals out			

Monthly Financial Goals

What improvements can be made from last month? ____________________

Goals For This Month:

1. ____________________
2. ____________________
3. ____________________

To reach these goals I need to:

- [ ] ____________________
- [ ] ____________________
- [ ] ____________________
- [ ] ____________________
- [ ] ____________________
- [ ] ____________________
- [ ] ____________________
- [ ] ____________________

Notes:

BUDGET at a GLANCE

INCOME SOURCE	AMOUNT	PAYMENT DATE	COMMENTS
INCOME TOTALS			

EXPENSES	AMOUNT	DUE DATE	COMMENTS
Housing			
mortgage/rent			
second mortgage			
property taxes			
home insurance			
maintenance/repairs			
alarm system			
Utilities			
electricity			
heat			
water/sewer			
garbage pick-up			
home phone			
internet			
cable/satellite			
cell phones			
Food			
groceries			
meals out			

Monthly Financial Goals

What improvements can be made from last month? ______________________

Goals For This Month:

1. ______________________
2. ______________________
3. ______________________

To reach these goals I need to:

- [ ] ______________________
- [ ] ______________________
- [ ] ______________________
- [ ] ______________________
- [ ] ______________________
- [ ] ______________________
- [ ] ______________________
- [ ] ______________________

Notes:

BUDGET at a GLANCE

INCOME SOURCE	AMOUNT	PAYMENT DATE	COMMENTS
INCOME TOTALS			

EXPENSES	AMOUNT	DUE DATE	COMMENTS
Housing			
mortgage/rent			
second mortgage			
property taxes			
home insurance			
maintenance/repairs			
alarm system			
Utilities			
electricity			
heat			
water/sewer			
garbage pick-up			
home phone			
internet			
cable/satellite			
cell phones			
Food			
groceries			
meals out			

Monthly Financial Goals

What improvements can be made from last month? ______________________

Goals For This Month:

1. ______________________
2. ______________________
3. ______________________

To reach these goals I need to:

- [ ] ______________________
- [ ] ______________________
- [ ] ______________________
- [ ] ______________________
- [ ] ______________________
- [ ] ______________________
- [ ] ______________________
- [ ] ______________________

Notes:

BUDGET at a GLANCE

INCOME SOURCE	AMOUNT	PAYMENT DATE	COMMENTS
INCOME TOTALS			

EXPENSES	AMOUNT	DUE DATE	COMMENTS
Housing			
mortgage/rent			
second mortgage			
property taxes			
home insurance			
maintenance/repairs			
alarm system			
Utilities			
electricity			
heat			
water/sewer			
garbage pick-up			
home phone			
internet			
cable/satellite			
cell phones			
Food			
groceries			
meals out			

Monthly Financial Goals

What improvements can be made from last month? ____________________

Goals For This Month:

1. ____________________
2. ____________________
3. ____________________

To reach these goals I need to:

- [ ] ____________________
- [ ] ____________________
- [ ] ____________________
- [ ] ____________________
- [ ] ____________________
- [ ] ____________________
- [ ] ____________________
- [ ] ____________________

Notes:

BUDGET at a GLANCE

INCOME SOURCE	AMOUNT	PAYMENT DATE	COMMENTS
INCOME TOTALS			

EXPENSES	AMOUNT	DUE DATE	COMMENTS
Housing			
mortgage/rent			
second mortgage			
property taxes			
home insurance			
maintenance/repairs			
alarm system			
Utilities			
electricity			
heat			
water/sewer			
garbage pick-up			
home phone			
internet			
cable/satellite			
cell phones			
Food			
groceries			
meals out			

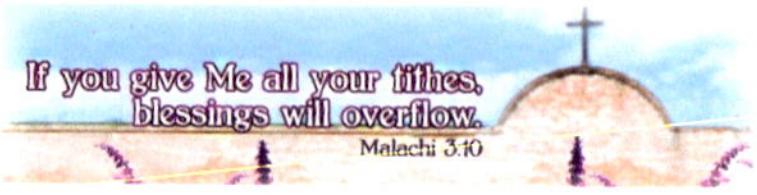

Monthly Financial Goals

What improvements can be made from last month? ____________________

Goals For This Month:

1. ____________________
2. ____________________
3. ____________________

To reach these goals I need to:

- [ ] ____________________
- [ ] ____________________
- [ ] ____________________
- [ ] ____________________
- [ ] ____________________
- [ ] ____________________
- [ ] ____________________
- [ ] ____________________

Notes:

BUDGET at a GLANCE

INCOME SOURCE	AMOUNT	PAYMENT DATE	COMMENTS
INCOME TOTALS			

EXPENSES	AMOUNT	DUE DATE	COMMENTS
Housing			
mortgage/rent			
second mortgage			
property taxes			
home insurance			
maintenance/repairs			
alarm system			
Utilities			
electricity			
heat			
water/sewer			
garbage pick-up			
home phone			
internet			
cable/satellite			
cell phones			
Food			
groceries			
meals out			

Monthly Financial Goals

What improvements can be made from last month? ______________________

Goals For This Month:

1. ______________________
2. ______________________
3. ______________________

To reach these goals I need to:

- [ ] ______________________
- [ ] ______________________
- [ ] ______________________
- [ ] ______________________
- [ ] ______________________
- [ ] ______________________
- [ ] ______________________
- [ ] ______________________

Notes:

BUDGET *at a* GLANCE

INCOME SOURCE	AMOUNT	PAYMENT DATE	COMMENTS
INCOME TOTALS			

EXPENSES	AMOUNT	DUE DATE	COMMENTS
Housing			
mortgage/rent			
second mortgage			
property taxes			
home insurance			
maintenance/repairs			
alarm system			
Utilities			
electricity			
heat			
water/sewer			
garbage pick-up			
home phone			
internet			
cable/satellite			
cell phones			
Food			
groceries			
meals out			

Monthly Financial Goals

What improvements can be made from last month? ______________________________

Goals For This Month:

1. ______________________________
2. ______________________________
3. ______________________________

To reach these goals I need to:

- [ ] ______________________________
- [ ] ______________________________
- [ ] ______________________________
- [ ] ______________________________
- [ ] ______________________________
- [ ] ______________________________
- [ ] ______________________________
- [ ] ______________________________

Notes:

BUDGET *at a* GLANCE

INCOME SOURCE	AMOUNT	PAYMENT DATE	COMMENTS
INCOME TOTALS			

EXPENSES	AMOUNT	DUE DATE	COMMENTS
Housing			
mortgage/rent			
second mortgage			
property taxes			
home insurance			
maintenance/repairs			
alarm system			
Utilities			
electricity			
heat			
water/sewer			
garbage pick-up			
home phone			
internet			
cable/satellite			
cell phones			
Food			
groceries			
meals out			

Monthly Financial Goals

What improvements can be made from last month? ______________________________

Goals For This Month:

1. ______________________________
2. ______________________________
3. ______________________________

To reach these goals I need to:

- [ ] ______________________________
- [ ] ______________________________
- [ ] ______________________________
- [ ] ______________________________
- [ ] ______________________________
- [ ] ______________________________
- [ ] ______________________________
- [ ] ______________________________

Notes:

BUDGET at a GLANCE

INCOME SOURCE	AMOUNT	PAYMENT DATE	COMMENTS
INCOME TOTALS			

EXPENSES	AMOUNT	DUE DATE	COMMENTS
Housing			
mortgage/rent			
second mortgage			
property taxes			
home insurance			
maintenance/repairs			
alarm system			
Utilities			
electricity			
heat			
water/sewer			
garbage pick-up			
home phone			
internet			
cable/satellite			
cell phones			
Food			
groceries			
meals out			

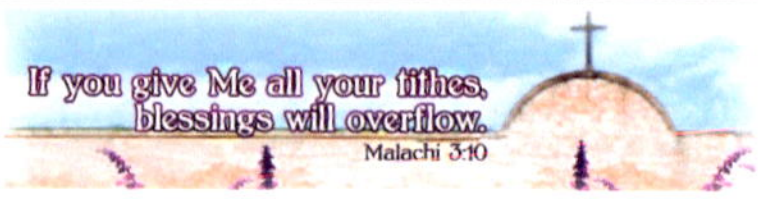

Monthly Financial Goals

What improvements can be made from last month? ____________________

Goals For This Month:

1. ____________________
2. ____________________
3. ____________________

To reach these goals I need to:

- [ ] ____________________
- [ ] ____________________
- [ ] ____________________
- [ ] ____________________
- [ ] ____________________
- [ ] ____________________
- [ ] ____________________
- [ ] ____________________

Notes:

BUDGET at a GLANCE

INCOME SOURCE	AMOUNT	PAYMENT DATE	COMMENTS
INCOME TOTALS			

EXPENSES	AMOUNT	DUE DATE	COMMENTS
Housing			
mortgage/rent			
second mortgage			
property taxes			
home insurance			
maintenance/repairs			
alarm system			
Utilities			
electricity			
heat			
water/sewer			
garbage pick-up			
home phone			
internet			
cable/satellite			
cell phones			
Food			
groceries			
meals out			

Monthly Financial Goals

What improvements can be made from last month? ____________________

Goals For This Month:

1. ____________________
2. ____________________
3. ____________________

To reach these goals I need to:

- [ ] ____________________
- [ ] ____________________
- [ ] ____________________
- [ ] ____________________
- [ ] ____________________
- [ ] ____________________
- [ ] ____________________
- [ ] ____________________

Notes:

BUDGET at a GLANCE

INCOME SOURCE	AMOUNT	PAYMENT DATE	COMMENTS
INCOME TOTALS			

EXPENSES	AMOUNT	DUE DATE	COMMENTS
Housing			
mortgage/rent			
second mortgage			
property taxes			
home insurance			
maintenance/repairs			
alarm system			
Utilities			
electricity			
heat			
water/sewer			
garbage pick-up			
home phone			
internet			
cable/satellite			
cell phones			
Food			
groceries			
meals out			

Monthly Financial Goals

What improvements can be made from last month? ____________________

Goals For This Month:

1. ____________________
2. ____________________
3. ____________________

To reach these goals I need to:

- [ ] ____________________
- [ ] ____________________
- [ ] ____________________
- [ ] ____________________
- [ ] ____________________
- [ ] ____________________
- [ ] ____________________
- [ ] ____________________

Notes:

BUDGET at a GLANCE

INCOME SOURCE	AMOUNT	PAYMENT DATE	COMMENTS
INCOME TOTALS			

EXPENSES	AMOUNT	DUE DATE	COMMENTS
Housing			
mortgage/rent			
second mortgage			
property taxes			
home insurance			
maintenance/repairs			
alarm system			
Utilities			
electricity			
heat			
water/sewer			
garbage pick-up			
home phone			
internet			
cable/satellite			
cell phones			
Food			
groceries			
meals out			

Monthly Financial Goals

What improvements can be made from last month? ____________________

Goals For This Month:

1. ____________________
2. ____________________
3. ____________________

To reach these goals I need to:

- [ ] ____________________
- [ ] ____________________
- [ ] ____________________
- [ ] ____________________
- [ ] ____________________
- [ ] ____________________
- [ ] ____________________
- [ ] ____________________

Notes:

BUDGET *at a* GLANCE

INCOME SOURCE	AMOUNT	PAYMENT DATE	COMMENTS
INCOME TOTALS			

EXPENSES	AMOUNT	DUE DATE	COMMENTS
Housing			
mortgage/rent			
second mortgage			
property taxes			
home insurance			
maintenance/repairs			
alarm system			
Utilities			
electricity			
heat			
water/sewer			
garbage pick-up			
home phone			
internet			
cable/satellite			
cell phones			
Food			
groceries			
meals out			

Monthly Financial Goals

What improvements can be made from last month? ______________________

Goals For This Month:

1. ______________________
2. ______________________
3. ______________________

To reach these goals I need to:

- [ ] ______________________
- [ ] ______________________
- [ ] ______________________
- [ ] ______________________
- [ ] ______________________
- [ ] ______________________
- [ ] ______________________
- [ ] ______________________

Notes:

BUDGET at a GLANCE

INCOME SOURCE	AMOUNT	PAYMENT DATE	COMMENTS
INCOME TOTALS			

EXPENSES	AMOUNT	DUE DATE	COMMENTS
Housing			
mortgage/rent			
second mortgage			
property taxes			
home insurance			
maintenance/repairs			
alarm system			
Utilities			
electricity			
heat			
water/sewer			
garbage pick-up			
home phone			
internet			
cable/satellite			
cell phones			
Food			
groceries			
meals out			

Monthly Financial Goals

What improvements can be made from last month? ________________________

Goals For This Month:

1. ________________________

2. ________________________

3. ________________________

To reach these goals I need to:

- [ ] ________________________
- [ ] ________________________
- [ ] ________________________
- [ ] ________________________
- [ ] ________________________
- [ ] ________________________
- [ ] ________________________
- [ ] ________________________

Notes:

BUDGET at a GLANCE

INCOME SOURCE	AMOUNT	PAYMENT DATE	COMMENTS
INCOME TOTALS			

EXPENSES	AMOUNT	DUE DATE	COMMENTS
Housing			
mortgage/rent			
second mortgage			
property taxes			
home insurance			
maintenance/repairs			
alarm system			
Utilities			
electricity			
heat			
water/sewer			
garbage pick-up			
home phone			
internet			
cable/satellite			
cell phones			
Food			
groceries			
meals out			

Monthly Financial Goals

What improvements can be made from last month? ____________________

Goals For This Month:

1. ____________________
2. ____________________
3. ____________________

To reach these goals I need to:

- [ ] ____________________
- [ ] ____________________
- [ ] ____________________
- [ ] ____________________
- [ ] ____________________
- [ ] ____________________
- [ ] ____________________
- [ ] ____________________

Notes:

BUDGET at a GLANCE

INCOME SOURCE	AMOUNT	PAYMENT DATE	COMMENTS
INCOME TOTALS			

EXPENSES	AMOUNT	DUE DATE	COMMENTS
Housing			
mortgage/rent			
second mortgage			
property taxes			
home insurance			
maintenance/repairs			
alarm system			
Utilities			
electricity			
heat			
water/sewer			
garbage pick-up			
home phone			
internet			
cable/satellite			
cell phones			
Food			
groceries			
meals out			

Monthly Financial Goals

What improvements can be made from last month? ______________________

Goals For This Month:

1. ______________________
2. ______________________
3. ______________________

To reach these goals I need to:

- ☐ ______________________
- ☐ ______________________
- ☐ ______________________
- ☐ ______________________
- ☐ ______________________
- ☐ ______________________
- ☐ ______________________
- ☐ ______________________

Notes:

BUDGET at a GLANCE

INCOME SOURCE	AMOUNT	PAYMENT DATE	COMMENTS
INCOME TOTALS			

EXPENSES	AMOUNT	DUE DATE	COMMENTS
Housing			
mortgage/rent			
second mortgage			
property taxes			
home insurance			
maintenance/repairs			
alarm system			
Utilities			
electricity			
heat			
water/sewer			
garbage pick-up			
home phone			
internet			
cable/satellite			
cell phones			
Food			
groceries			
meals out			

Monthly Financial Goals

What improvements can be made from last month? ______________________

Goals For This Month:

1. ______________________
2. ______________________
3. ______________________

To reach these goals I need to:

- [ ] ______________________
- [ ] ______________________
- [ ] ______________________
- [ ] ______________________
- [ ] ______________________
- [ ] ______________________
- [ ] ______________________
- [ ] ______________________

Notes:

BUDGET at a GLANCE

INCOME SOURCE	AMOUNT	PAYMENT DATE	COMMENTS
INCOME TOTALS			

EXPENSES	AMOUNT	DUE DATE	COMMENTS
Housing			
mortgage/rent			
second mortgage			
property taxes			
home insurance			
maintenance/repairs			
alarm system			
Utilities			
electricity			
heat			
water/sewer			
garbage pick-up			
home phone			
internet			
cable/satellite			
cell phones			
Food			
groceries			
meals out			

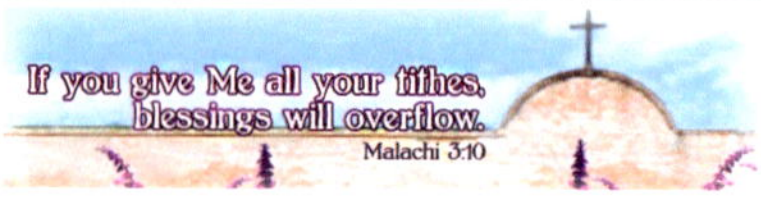

Monthly Financial Goals

What improvements can be made from last month? ____________________

Goals For This Month:

1. ____________________
2. ____________________
3. ____________________

To reach these goals I need to:

- [ ] ____________________
- [ ] ____________________
- [ ] ____________________
- [ ] ____________________
- [ ] ____________________
- [ ] ____________________
- [ ] ____________________
- [ ] ____________________

Notes:

BUDGET *at a* GLANCE

INCOME SOURCE	AMOUNT	PAYMENT DATE	COMMENTS
INCOME TOTALS			

EXPENSES	AMOUNT	DUE DATE	COMMENTS
Housing			
mortgage/rent			
second mortgage			
property taxes			
home insurance			
maintenance/repairs			
alarm system			
Utilities			
electricity			
heat			
water/sewer			
garbage pick-up			
home phone			
internet			
cable/satellite			
cell phones			
Food			
groceries			
meals out			

Monthly Financial Goals

What improvements can be made from last month? ______________________

Goals For This Month:

1. ______________________
2. ______________________
3. ______________________

To reach these goals I need to:

- [ ] ______________________
- [ ] ______________________
- [ ] ______________________
- [ ] ______________________
- [ ] ______________________
- [ ] ______________________
- [ ] ______________________
- [ ] ______________________

Notes:

BUDGET at a GLANCE

INCOME SOURCE	AMOUNT	PAYMENT DATE	COMMENTS
INCOME TOTALS			

EXPENSES	AMOUNT	DUE DATE	COMMENTS
Housing			
mortgage/rent			
second mortgage			
property taxes			
home insurance			
maintenance/repairs			
alarm system			
Utilities			
electricity			
heat			
water/sewer			
garbage pick-up			
home phone			
internet			
cable/satellite			
cell phones			
Food			
groceries			
meals out			

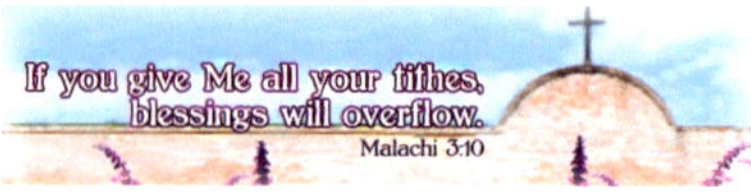

Monthly Financial Goals

What improvements can be made from last month? ____________________

Goals For This Month:

1. ____________________
2. ____________________
3. ____________________

To reach these goals I need to:

- [ ] ____________________
- [ ] ____________________
- [ ] ____________________
- [ ] ____________________
- [ ] ____________________
- [ ] ____________________
- [ ] ____________________
- [ ] ____________________

Notes:

BUDGET at a GLANCE

INCOME SOURCE	AMOUNT	PAYMENT DATE	COMMENTS
INCOME TOTALS			

EXPENSES	AMOUNT	DUE DATE	COMMENTS
Housing			
mortgage/rent			
second mortgage			
property taxes			
home insurance			
maintenance/repairs			
alarm system			
Utilities			
electricity			
heat			
water/sewer			
garbage pick-up			
home phone			
internet			
cable/satellite			
cell phones			
Food			
groceries			
meals out			

Monthly Financial Goals

What improvements can be made from last month? ______________________

Goals For This Month:

1. ______________________
2. ______________________
3. ______________________

To reach these goals I need to:

- [ ] ______________________
- [ ] ______________________
- [ ] ______________________
- [ ] ______________________
- [ ] ______________________
- [ ] ______________________
- [ ] ______________________
- [ ] ______________________

Notes:

BUDGET at a GLANCE

INCOME SOURCE	AMOUNT	PAYMENT DATE	COMMENTS
INCOME TOTALS			

EXPENSES	AMOUNT	DUE DATE	COMMENTS
Housing			
mortgage/rent			
second mortgage			
property taxes			
home insurance			
maintenance/repairs			
alarm system			
Utilities			
electricity			
heat			
water/sewer			
garbage pick-up			
home phone			
internet			
cable/satellite			
cell phones			
Food			
groceries			
meals out			

Monthly Financial Goals

What improvements can be made from last month? ______________________

Goals For This Month:

1. ______________________
2. ______________________
3. ______________________

To reach these goals I need to:

- [ ] ______________________
- [ ] ______________________
- [ ] ______________________
- [ ] ______________________
- [ ] ______________________
- [ ] ______________________
- [ ] ______________________
- [ ] ______________________

Notes:

BUDGET at a GLANCE

INCOME SOURCE	AMOUNT	PAYMENT DATE	COMMENTS
INCOME TOTALS			

EXPENSES	AMOUNT	DUE DATE	COMMENTS
Housing			
mortgage/rent			
second mortgage			
property taxes			
home insurance			
maintenance/repairs			
alarm system			
Utilities			
electricity			
heat			
water/sewer			
garbage pick-up			
home phone			
internet			
cable/satellite			
cell phones			
Food			
groceries			
meals out			

Monthly Financial Goals

What improvements can be made from last month? ______________________

Goals For This Month:

1. ______________________
2. ______________________
3. ______________________

To reach these goals I need to:

- [ ] ______________________
- [ ] ______________________
- [ ] ______________________
- [ ] ______________________
- [ ] ______________________
- [ ] ______________________
- [ ] ______________________
- [ ] ______________________

Notes:

BUDGET at a GLANCE

INCOME SOURCE	AMOUNT	PAYMENT DATE	COMMENTS
INCOME TOTALS			

EXPENSES	AMOUNT	DUE DATE	COMMENTS
Housing			
mortgage/rent			
second mortgage			
property taxes			
home insurance			
maintenance/repairs			
alarm system			
Utilities			
electricity			
heat			
water/sewer			
garbage pick-up			
home phone			
internet			
cable/satellite			
cell phones			
Food			
groceries			
meals out			

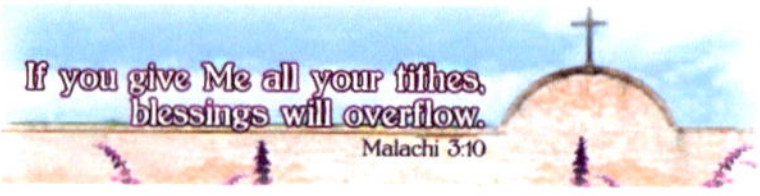

Monthly Financial Goals

What improvements can be made from last month? ______________________________

Goals For This Month:

1. ______________________________
2. ______________________________
3. ______________________________

To reach these goals I need to:

- [ ] ______________________________
- [ ] ______________________________
- [ ] ______________________________
- [ ] ______________________________
- [ ] ______________________________
- [ ] ______________________________
- [ ] ______________________________
- [ ] ______________________________

Notes:

BUDGET at a GLANCE

INCOME SOURCE	AMOUNT	PAYMENT DATE	COMMENTS
INCOME TOTALS			

EXPENSES	AMOUNT	DUE DATE	COMMENTS
Housing			
mortgage/rent			
second mortgage			
property taxes			
home insurance			
maintenance/repairs			
alarm system			
Utilities			
electricity			
heat			
water/sewer			
garbage pick-up			
home phone			
internet			
cable/satellite			
cell phones			
Food			
groceries			
meals out			

Monthly Financial Goals

What improvements can be made from last month? ____________________

Goals For This Month:

1. ____________________
2. ____________________
3. ____________________

To reach these goals I need to:

- [ ] ____________________
- [ ] ____________________
- [ ] ____________________
- [ ] ____________________
- [ ] ____________________
- [ ] ____________________
- [ ] ____________________
- [ ] ____________________

Notes:

BUDGET at a GLANCE

INCOME SOURCE	AMOUNT	PAYMENT DATE	COMMENTS
INCOME TOTALS			

EXPENSES	AMOUNT	DUE DATE	COMMENTS
Housing			
mortgage/rent			
second mortgage			
property taxes			
home insurance			
maintenance/repairs			
alarm system			
Utilities			
electricity			
heat			
water/sewer			
garbage pick-up			
home phone			
internet			
cable/satellite			
cell phones			
Food			
groceries			
meals out			

Monthly Financial Goals

What improvements can be made from last month? ______________________

Goals For This Month:

1. ______________________
2. ______________________
3. ______________________

To reach these goals I need to:

- [ ] ______________________
- [ ] ______________________
- [ ] ______________________
- [ ] ______________________
- [ ] ______________________
- [ ] ______________________
- [ ] ______________________
- [ ] ______________________

Notes:

BUDGET at a GLANCE

INCOME SOURCE	AMOUNT	PAYMENT DATE	COMMENTS
INCOME TOTALS			

EXPENSES	AMOUNT	DUE DATE	COMMENTS
Housing			
mortgage/rent			
second mortgage			
property taxes			
home insurance			
maintenance/repairs			
alarm system			
Utilities			
electricity			
heat			
water/sewer			
garbage pick-up			
home phone			
internet			
cable/satellite			
cell phones			
Food			
groceries			
meals out			

Monthly Financial Goals

What improvements can be made from last month? ____________________

Goals For This Month:

1. ____________________
2. ____________________
3. ____________________

To reach these goals I need to:

- [ ] ____________________
- [ ] ____________________
- [ ] ____________________
- [ ] ____________________
- [ ] ____________________
- [ ] ____________________
- [ ] ____________________
- [ ] ____________________

Notes:

BUDGET at a GLANCE

INCOME SOURCE	AMOUNT	PAYMENT DATE	COMMENTS
INCOME TOTALS			

EXPENSES	AMOUNT	DUE DATE	COMMENTS
Housing			
mortgage/rent			
second mortgage			
property taxes			
home insurance			
maintenance/repairs			
alarm system			
Utilities			
electricity			
heat			
water/sewer			
garbage pick-up			
home phone			
internet			
cable/satellite			
cell phones			
Food			
groceries			
meals out			

Monthly Financial Goals

What improvements can be made from last month? ______________________

Goals For This Month:

1. ______________________
2. ______________________
3. ______________________

To reach these goals I need to:

- [ ] ______________________
- [ ] ______________________
- [ ] ______________________
- [ ] ______________________
- [ ] ______________________
- [ ] ______________________
- [ ] ______________________
- [ ] ______________________

Notes:

BUDGET at a GLANCE

INCOME SOURCE	AMOUNT	PAYMENT DATE	COMMENTS
INCOME TOTALS			

EXPENSES	AMOUNT	DUE DATE	COMMENTS
Housing			
mortgage/rent			
second mortgage			
property taxes			
home insurance			
maintenance/repairs			
alarm system			
Utilities			
electricity			
heat			
water/sewer			
garbage pick-up			
home phone			
internet			
cable/satellite			
cell phones			
Food			
groceries			
meals out			

Monthly Financial Goals

What improvements can be made from last month? ______________________________

Goals For This Month:

1. ______________________________
2. ______________________________
3. ______________________________

To reach these goals I need to:

- [ ] ______________________________
- [ ] ______________________________
- [ ] ______________________________
- [ ] ______________________________
- [ ] ______________________________
- [ ] ______________________________
- [ ] ______________________________
- [ ] ______________________________

Notes:

BUDGET *at a* GLANCE

INCOME SOURCE	AMOUNT	PAYMENT DATE	COMMENTS
INCOME TOTALS			

EXPENSES	AMOUNT	DUE DATE	COMMENTS
Housing			
mortgage/rent			
second mortgage			
property taxes			
home insurance			
maintenance/repairs			
alarm system			
Utilities			
electricity			
heat			
water/sewer			
garbage pick-up			
home phone			
internet			
cable/satellite			
cell phones			
Food			
groceries			
meals out			

Monthly Financial Goals

What improvements can be made from last month? ______________________

Goals For This Month:

1. ______________________
2. ______________________
3. ______________________

To reach these goals I need to:

- [ ] ______________________
- [ ] ______________________
- [ ] ______________________
- [ ] ______________________
- [ ] ______________________
- [ ] ______________________
- [ ] ______________________
- [ ] ______________________

Notes:

BUDGET at a GLANCE

INCOME SOURCE	AMOUNT	PAYMENT DATE	COMMENTS
INCOME TOTALS			

EXPENSES	AMOUNT	DUE DATE	COMMENTS
Housing			
mortgage/rent			
second mortgage			
property taxes			
home insurance			
maintenance/repairs			
alarm system			
Utilities			
electricity			
heat			
water/sewer			
garbage pick-up			
home phone			
internet			
cable/satellite			
cell phones			
Food			
groceries			
meals out			

Monthly Financial Goals

What improvements can be made from last month? ____________________

Goals For This Month:

1. ____________________
2. ____________________
3. ____________________

To reach these goals I need to:

- [ ] ____________________
- [ ] ____________________
- [ ] ____________________
- [ ] ____________________
- [ ] ____________________
- [ ] ____________________
- [ ] ____________________
- [ ] ____________________

Notes:

BUDGET at a GLANCE

INCOME SOURCE	AMOUNT	PAYMENT DATE	COMMENTS
INCOME TOTALS			

EXPENSES	AMOUNT	DUE DATE	COMMENTS
Housing			
mortgage/rent			
second mortgage			
property taxes			
home insurance			
maintenance/repairs			
alarm system			
Utilities			
electricity			
heat			
water/sewer			
garbage pick-up			
home phone			
internet			
cable/satellite			
cell phones			
Food			
groceries			
meals out			

Monthly Financial Goals

What improvements can be made from last month? ____________________

Goals For This Month:

1. ____________________
2. ____________________
3. ____________________

To reach these goals I need to:

- [ ] ____________________
- [ ] ____________________
- [ ] ____________________
- [ ] ____________________
- [ ] ____________________
- [ ] ____________________
- [ ] ____________________
- [ ] ____________________

Notes:

BUDGET at a GLANCE

INCOME SOURCE	AMOUNT	PAYMENT DATE	COMMENTS
INCOME TOTALS			

EXPENSES	AMOUNT	DUE DATE	COMMENTS
Housing			
mortgage/rent			
second mortgage			
property taxes			
home insurance			
maintenance/repairs			
alarm system			
Utilities			
electricity			
heat			
water/sewer			
garbage pick-up			
home phone			
internet			
cable/satellite			
cell phones			
Food			
groceries			
meals out			

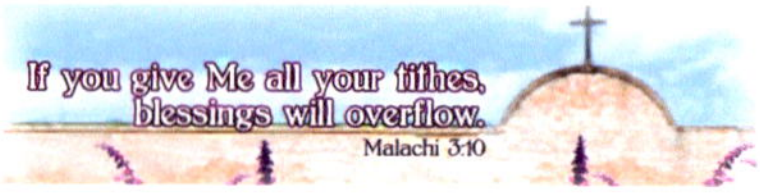

Monthly Financial Goals

What improvements can be made from last month? ____________________

Goals For This Month:

1. ____________________
2. ____________________
3. ____________________

To reach these goals I need to:

- [ ] ____________________
- [ ] ____________________
- [ ] ____________________
- [ ] ____________________
- [ ] ____________________
- [ ] ____________________
- [ ] ____________________
- [ ] ____________________

Notes:

BUDGET at a GLANCE

INCOME SOURCE	AMOUNT	PAYMENT DATE	COMMENTS
INCOME TOTALS			

EXPENSES	AMOUNT	DUE DATE	COMMENTS
Housing			
mortgage/rent			
second mortgage			
property taxes			
home insurance			
maintenance/repairs			
alarm system			
Utilities			
electricity			
heat			
water/sewer			
garbage pick-up			
home phone			
internet			
cable/satellite			
cell phones			
Food			
groceries			
meals out			

Monthly Financial Goals

What improvements can be made from last month? ____________________

Goals For This Month:

1. ____________________
2. ____________________
3. ____________________

To reach these goals I need to:

- [ ] ____________________
- [ ] ____________________
- [ ] ____________________
- [ ] ____________________
- [ ] ____________________
- [ ] ____________________
- [ ] ____________________
- [ ] ____________________

Notes:

BUDGET at a GLANCE

INCOME SOURCE	AMOUNT	PAYMENT DATE	COMMENTS
INCOME TOTALS			

EXPENSES	AMOUNT	DUE DATE	COMMENTS
Housing			
mortgage/rent			
second mortgage			
property taxes			
home insurance			
maintenance/repairs			
alarm system			
Utilities			
electricity			
heat			
water/sewer			
garbage pick-up			
home phone			
internet			
cable/satellite			
cell phones			
Food			
groceries			
meals out			

Monthly Financial Goals

What improvements can be made from last month? ______________________

Goals For This Month:

1. ______________________
2. ______________________
3. ______________________

To reach these goals I need to:

- [ ] ______________________
- [ ] ______________________
- [ ] ______________________
- [ ] ______________________
- [ ] ______________________
- [ ] ______________________
- [ ] ______________________
- [ ] ______________________

Notes:

BUDGET *at a* GLANCE

INCOME SOURCE	AMOUNT	PAYMENT DATE	COMMENTS
INCOME TOTALS			

EXPENSES	AMOUNT	DUE DATE	COMMENTS
Housing			
mortgage/rent			
second mortgage			
property taxes			
home insurance			
maintenance/repairs			
alarm system			
Utilities			
electricity			
heat			
water/sewer			
garbage pick-up			
home phone			
internet			
cable/satellite			
cell phones			
Food			
groceries			
meals out			

Monthly Financial Goals

What improvements can be made from last month? ____________________

Goals For This Month:

1. ____________________
2. ____________________
3. ____________________

To reach these goals I need to:

- [ ] ____________________
- [ ] ____________________
- [ ] ____________________
- [ ] ____________________
- [ ] ____________________
- [ ] ____________________
- [ ] ____________________
- [ ] ____________________

Notes:

BUDGET at a GLANCE

INCOME SOURCE	AMOUNT	PAYMENT DATE	COMMENTS
INCOME TOTALS			

EXPENSES	AMOUNT	DUE DATE	COMMENTS
Housing			
mortgage/rent			
second mortgage			
property taxes			
home insurance			
maintenance/repairs			
alarm system			
Utilities			
electricity			
heat			
water/sewer			
garbage pick-up			
home phone			
internet			
cable/satellite			
cell phones			
Food			
groceries			
meals out			

Monthly Financial Goals

What improvements can be made from last month? ____________________

Goals For This Month:

1. ____________________
2. ____________________
3. ____________________

To reach these goals I need to:

- [ ] ____________________
- [ ] ____________________
- [ ] ____________________
- [ ] ____________________
- [ ] ____________________
- [ ] ____________________
- [ ] ____________________
- [ ] ____________________

Notes:

BUDGET at a GLANCE

INCOME SOURCE	AMOUNT	PAYMENT DATE	COMMENTS
INCOME TOTALS			

EXPENSES	AMOUNT	DUE DATE	COMMENTS
Housing			
mortgage/rent			
second mortgage			
property taxes			
home insurance			
maintenance/repairs			
alarm system			
Utilities			
electricity			
heat			
water/sewer			
garbage pick-up			
home phone			
internet			
cable/satellite			
cell phones			
Food			
groceries			
meals out			

Monthly Financial Goals

What improvements can be made from last month? ______________________________

Goals For This Month:

1. ______________________________
2. ______________________________
3. ______________________________

To reach these goals I need to:

- [ ] ______________________________
- [ ] ______________________________
- [ ] ______________________________
- [ ] ______________________________
- [ ] ______________________________
- [ ] ______________________________
- [ ] ______________________________
- [ ] ______________________________

Notes:

BUDGET at a GLANCE

INCOME SOURCE	AMOUNT	PAYMENT DATE	COMMENTS
INCOME TOTALS			

EXPENSES	AMOUNT	DUE DATE	COMMENTS
Housing			
mortgage/rent			
second mortgage			
property taxes			
home insurance			
maintenance/repairs			
alarm system			
Utilities			
electricity			
heat			
water/sewer			
garbage pick-up			
home phone			
internet			
cable/satellite			
cell phones			
Food			
groceries			
meals out			

Monthly Financial Goals

What improvements can be made from last month? ______________________

Goals For This Month:

1. ______________________
2. ______________________
3. ______________________

To reach these goals I need to:

- ☐ ______________________
- ☐ ______________________
- ☐ ______________________
- ☐ ______________________
- ☐ ______________________
- ☐ ______________________
- ☐ ______________________
- ☐ ______________________

Notes:

BUDGET at a GLANCE

INCOME SOURCE	AMOUNT	PAYMENT DATE	COMMENTS
INCOME TOTALS			

EXPENSES	AMOUNT	DUE DATE	COMMENTS
Housing			
mortgage/rent			
second mortgage			
property taxes			
home insurance			
maintenance/repairs			
alarm system			
Utilities			
electricity			
heat			
water/sewer			
garbage pick-up			
home phone			
internet			
cable/satellite			
cell phones			
Food			
groceries			
meals out			

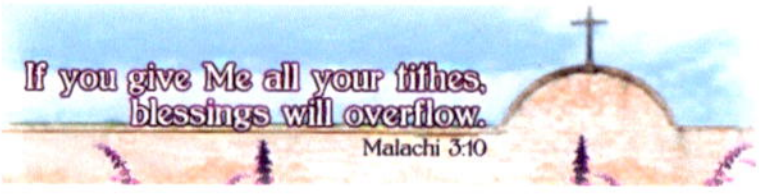

Monthly Financial Goals

What improvements can be made from last month? ____________________

Goals For This Month:

1. ____________________
2. ____________________
3. ____________________

To reach these goals I need to:

- ☐ ____________________
- ☐ ____________________
- ☐ ____________________
- ☐ ____________________
- ☐ ____________________
- ☐ ____________________
- ☐ ____________________
- ☐ ____________________

Notes:

BUDGET at a GLANCE

INCOME SOURCE	AMOUNT	PAYMENT DATE	COMMENTS
INCOME TOTALS			

EXPENSES	AMOUNT	DUE DATE	COMMENTS
Housing			
mortgage/rent			
second mortgage			
property taxes			
home insurance			
maintenance/repairs			
alarm system			
Utilities			
electricity			
heat			
water/sewer			
garbage pick-up			
home phone			
internet			
cable/satellite			
cell phones			
Food			
groceries			
meals out			

Monthly Financial Goals

What improvements can be made from last month? ____________________

Goals For This Month:

1. ____________________
2. ____________________
3. ____________________

To reach these goals I need to:

- [ ] ____________________
- [ ] ____________________
- [ ] ____________________
- [ ] ____________________
- [ ] ____________________
- [ ] ____________________
- [ ] ____________________
- [ ] ____________________

Notes:

BUDGET at a GLANCE

INCOME SOURCE	AMOUNT	PAYMENT DATE	COMMENTS
INCOME TOTALS			

EXPENSES	AMOUNT	DUE DATE	COMMENTS
Housing			
mortgage/rent			
second mortgage			
property taxes			
home insurance			
maintenance/repairs			
alarm system			
Utilities			
electricity			
heat			
water/sewer			
garbage pick-up			
home phone			
internet			
cable/satellite			
cell phones			
Food			
groceries			
meals out			

Monthly Financial Goals

What improvements can be made from last month? ____________________

Goals For This Month:

1. ____________________
2. ____________________
3. ____________________

To reach these goals I need to:

- [ ] ____________________
- [ ] ____________________
- [ ] ____________________
- [ ] ____________________
- [ ] ____________________
- [ ] ____________________
- [ ] ____________________
- [ ] ____________________

Notes:

BUDGET at a GLANCE

INCOME SOURCE	AMOUNT	PAYMENT DATE	COMMENTS
INCOME TOTALS			

EXPENSES	AMOUNT	DUE DATE	COMMENTS
Housing			
mortgage/rent			
second mortgage			
property taxes			
home insurance			
maintenance/repairs			
alarm system			
Utilities			
electricity			
heat			
water/sewer			
garbage pick-up			
home phone			
internet			
cable/satellite			
cell phones			
Food			
groceries			
meals out			

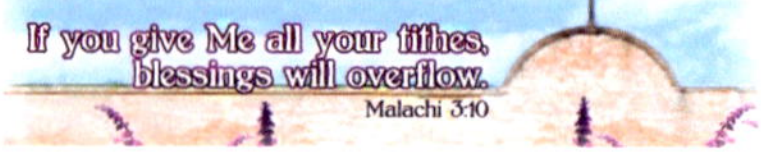

Monthly Financial Goals

What improvements can be made from last month? ____________________

Goals For This Month:

1. ____________________
2. ____________________
3. ____________________

To reach these goals I need to:

- [ ] ____________________
- [ ] ____________________
- [ ] ____________________
- [ ] ____________________
- [ ] ____________________
- [ ] ____________________
- [ ] ____________________
- [ ] ____________________

Notes:

BUDGET at a GLANCE

INCOME SOURCE	AMOUNT	PAYMENT DATE	COMMENTS
INCOME TOTALS			

EXPENSES	AMOUNT	DUE DATE	COMMENTS
Housing			
mortgage/rent			
second mortgage			
property taxes			
home insurance			
maintenance/repairs			
alarm system			
Utilities			
electricity			
heat			
water/sewer			
garbage pick-up			
home phone			
internet			
cable/satellite			
cell phones			
Food			
groceries			
meals out			

Made in the USA
Las Vegas, NV
03 November 2026

57425080R00145